Cybersecurity Governance
A Boardroom Blueprint

Victor M. Font Jr.

CYBERSECURITY
GOVERNANCE
A BOARDROOM BLUEPRINT

Copyright

Publisher

A FontLife Publication, LLC

United States of America

First Edition

2026

ISBN

ISBN (Print): 978-1-62422-061-6

ISBN (eBook): 978-1-62422-062-3

Disclaimer

This book is intended for educational and informational purposes only. It does not constitute legal advice, regulatory advice, financial advice, or professional consulting services. While the author has made every effort to ensure the accuracy and completeness of the information contained herein, laws, regulations, standards, and enforcement practices change over time and may vary by jurisdiction.

Readers are encouraged to consult qualified legal, regulatory, audit, or cybersecurity professionals regarding their specific circumstances.

Neither the author nor the publisher assumes any liability for actions taken or not taken based on the information contained in this book.

Governance and Standards Notice

References to cybersecurity frameworks, standards, regulations, and case law—including but not limited to NIST, ISO, SEC, DOJ, FTC, and judicial decisions—are provided for illustrative and educational purposes. Inclusion of these references does not imply endorsement by any governmental or standards-setting body.

This publication is framework-agnostic and does not require compliance with any single standard unless otherwise mandated by applicable law or regulation.

AI-Generated Content Disclosure

Certain visual elements associated with this publication, where applicable, may include AI-generated images used for illustrative or design purposes. No AI-generated content has been used to fabricate legal authorities, regulatory guidance, or factual case law referenced in this work.

Trademarks

Printing and Distribution

Printed in the United States of America

Distributed by A FontLife Publication, LLC

Contents

Cybersecurity, Fiduciary Duty, and the Modern Board 1

Why This Book Exists and How It Should Be Used...........5

Part I: Cybersecurity as a Governance Obligation 9

Chapter 1: The End of Cybersecurity as a Technical Problem 10

Chapter 2: Cyber Risk as Enterprise Risk 13

Chapter 3: Fiduciary Duty in the Cyber Age 17

Chapter 4: Cybersecurity and Mission Failure 20

Part II: Governance Architecture for Cybersecurity.......23

Chapter 5: Governing Versus Managing Cybersecurity 24

Chapter 6: The Cybersecurity Governance Model..... 27

Chapter 7: Roles, Responsibilities, and Authority 30

Chapter 8: Committees, Charters, and Reporting Discipline..........33

Chapter 9: Information Flow, Escalation, and Decision Rights..........36

Chapter 10: Governance Failure Modes and Structural Warning Signs..........39

Closing of Part II 41

Part III: Cyber Risk as a Board-Level System 42

Chapter 11: Framing Cyber Risk for Leadership Decision-Making 43

Chapter 12: Risk Appetite, Tolerance, and the Limits of Security 46

Chapter 13: Enterprise Cyber Risk Assessment as a Governance Tool 49

Chapter 14: Risk Treatment, Acceptance, and Governance Discipline 52

Chapter 15: Cybersecurity Investment as Risk Governance 55

Chapter 16: Risk Ownership, Accountability, and Escalation 57

Closing of Part III 59

Part IV: Policy as a Governance Instrument 60

Chapter 17: Policy as an Instrument of Governance, Not Administration 61

Chapter 18: Policy Hierarchy, Authority, and Board Ownership 64

Chapter 19: Core Cybersecurity Governance Policies 67

Chapter 20: Policy as Evidence of Due Diligence......70

Chapter 21: Policy Lifecycle Management and Governance Drift......72

Chapter 22: Exceptions, Enforcement, and Governance Integrity......74

Closing of Part IV......76

Part V: Assurance, Oversight, and Continuous Monitoring......78

Chapter 23: Assurance Versus Activity: Knowing the Difference......79

Chapter 24: Independent Validation and the Role of Assurance Functions......82

Chapter 25: Management Review, Internal Audit, and Board Oversight......84

Chapter 26: Metrics That Inform Governance, Not Noise......86

Chapter 27: Continuous Monitoring as a Governance Feedback Loop......89

Chapter 28: Escalation, Transparency, and the Courage to Surface Bad News......91

Closing of Part V......93

Part VI: Incident Preparedness and Leadership Decision-Making 94

Chapter 29: Cyber Incidents as Organizational Crises 95

Chapter 30: Preparedness as a Governance Responsibility 98

Chapter 31: Executive Authority, Escalation, and Decision Rights During Incidents 100

Chapter 32: The Board's Role During a Cyber Incident 102

Chapter 33: Legal, Regulatory, and Disclosure Considerations 105

Chapter 34: Tabletop Exercises as Governance Validation 108

Chapter 35: Post-Incident Review and Governance Learning 110

Closing of Part VI 112

Part VII: Third-Party, Vendor, and Ecosystem Risk 114

Chapter 36: The Myth of the Organizational Boundary 115

Chapter 37: Extended Enterprise Risk as a Governance Concern 117

Chapter 38: Due Diligence Beyond the Checkbox ...119
Chapter 39: Contractual Controls and the Limits of Paper Governance 121
Chapter 40: Ongoing Monitoring and the Illusion of Static Risk 123
Chapter 41: Concentration, Dependency, and Exit Risk 125
Chapter 42: Accountability for Third-Party Risk Governance 127
Closing of Part VII 129
Part VIII: Culture, Ethics, and Organizational Resilience 131
Chapter 43: Cybersecurity Culture as a Board Responsibility 132
Chapter 44: Tone at the Top and Behavioral Signals 134
Chapter 45: Ethics, Data Stewardship, and Moral Obligation 136
Chapter 46: Privacy, Trust, and the Social License to Operate 138
Chapter 47: Psychological Safety, Reporting, and the Prevention of Silence 140

Chapter 48: Resilience as a Cultural and Governance Outcome 142
Closing of Part VIII 144

Part IX: Maturity, Strategic Evolution, and the Future of Cybersecurity Governance 145

Chapter 49: The Illusion of Cybersecurity Maturity 146
Chapter 50: Maturity Models as Governance Tools, Not Scorecards 148
Chapter 51: Governance Drift and the Slow Erosion of Oversight 150
Chapter 52: Strategic Roadmapping for Cybersecurity Governance 152
Chapter 53: Board Education and the Continuity of Oversight 154
Chapter 54: Preparing for the Future Board Environment 156
Closing of Part IX 158

Part X The Board's Cybersecurity Playbook 160

Chapter 55: What Good Cybersecurity Governance Actually Looks Like 161
Chapter 56: The Board's Standing Responsibilities in Cybersecurity Oversight 164

Chapter 57: Questions Effective Boards Ask—and Insist On Answering 166

Chapter 58: Cybersecurity as an Enduring Board Discipline 168

Chapter 59: Defensibility, Not Perfection 170

Chapter 60: Governing in an Insecure World 172

From Obligation to Practice 174

References and Citations 176

Regulatory Alignment Matrix 186

Jurisdiction-Specific Addenda 198

Addendum A: Nonprofit Organizations 199

Addendum B: Healthcare Organizations 204

Addendum C: Financial Services 208

Addendum D: Public Sector and Government-Adjacent Organizations 212

Cybersecurity, Fiduciary Duty, and the Modern Board

Boards of Directors are no strangers to risk. Financial uncertainty, regulatory complexity, operational disruption, and reputational exposure have long been within the Board's remit. What has changed—decisively and permanently—is the role cybersecurity now plays in shaping all of those risks simultaneously.

Cybersecurity is no longer an issue that can be responsibly delegated and periodically reviewed. It is now a standing governance obligation. Regulators, courts, insurers, investors, donors, and the public increasingly evaluate cyber incidents not by asking whether an organization was attacked, but whether its leadership exercised informed, disciplined, and documented oversight.

That shift places Boards squarely at the center of cybersecurity governance.

This book arrives at a moment when many Directors sense this responsibility but lack a coherent framework for exercising it. Too often, cybersecurity is presented to Boards as a technical briefing, a compliance checklist, or a crisis after the fact. What is missing is a governance-first articulation—one that respects the Board's role, acknowledges the limits of prediction, and emphasizes accountability, decision-making, and stewardship.

Cybersecurity as a Governance Responsibility fills that gap.

Rather than offering tools, tactics, or vendor prescriptions, this work focuses on the elements Boards are uniquely positioned to govern: authority, structure, risk appetite, policy, assurance, culture, and leadership conduct under pressure. It treats cybersecurity not as an engineering problem to be solved, but as an enduring governance discipline to be exercised.

This is not a book about perfect security. No such condition exists. It is a book about defensible governance—about what it means for Boards to act reasonably, deliberately, and transparently in an environment where cyber risk is unavoidable.

Directors who engage seriously with this framework will find it both clarifying and challenging. It asks Boards to accept cybersecurity as part of their fiduciary identity, not an uncomfortable add-on. It demands rigor, documentation, and continuous attention. And it offers something increasingly rare in the cybersecurity discourse: a way forward that aligns responsibility with authority.

For Boards seeking to govern, rather than merely react, this book is a necessary contribution.

A three-tier architectural diagram: Top: Board Oversight, Middle: Executive Accountability, Bottom: Operational Execution

Why This Book Exists and How It Should Be Used

This book was written because too many cybersecurity failures are not technical failures at all. They are governance failures.

Over the past decade, cybersecurity has been framed primarily as a problem of tools, expertise, and implementation. Organizations have invested heavily in technology, consultants, and compliance programs, yet incidents continue to escalate in frequency and impact. When failures occur, the familiar refrain follows: the threat was sophisticated, the attack was unprecedented, the outcome was unavoidable.

Increasingly, regulators and courts are unconvinced.

The question being asked has changed. It is no longer *"Why did the breach occur?"* but *"Where was governance?"*

Boards are now expected to understand cyber risk as enterprise risk, to oversee it with the same discipline applied to financial controls and legal compliance, and to demonstrate that oversight through structure, documentation, and decision-making. Many Directors recognize this expectation intuitively, but lack a clear, role-appropriate framework for meeting it.

This book is that framework.

It is not a technical manual. It does not teach readers how to configure systems or respond to malware. It is written expressly for Boards and organizational leadership, using the language of governance rather than engineering.

The structure of the book reflects that intent. It begins by establishing cybersecurity as a fiduciary and governance obligation, then moves deliberately through governance architecture, risk decision systems, policy authority, assurance mechanisms, crisis leadership, third-party exposure, culture, maturity, and long-term stewardship. Each section builds on the last, because governance itself is cumulative.

This book is designed to be used, not merely read.

Boards may use it to:

- frame cybersecurity oversight discussions,
- shape committee charters and reporting expectations,
- evaluate management readiness,
- guide policy adoption and assurance planning,
- prepare for regulatory or audit scrutiny,
- educate new Directors on cybersecurity governance responsibilities.

Executives may use it to:

- align cybersecurity strategy with Board expectations,
- clarify accountability and escalation,

- structure reporting and assurance,
- prepare leadership for crisis decision-making.

Advisors, auditors, and regulators may use it as a reference point for what reasonable cybersecurity governance looks like in practice.

This book does not promise certainty. Cybersecurity does not allow it. What it offers instead is clarity—clarity of role, clarity of responsibility, and clarity of expectation.

In an insecure world, that clarity is not optional. It is the foundation of responsible leadership.

PART I:

CYBERSECURITY AS A GOVERNANCE OBLIGATION

Chapter 1: The End of Cybersecurity as a Technical Problem

For decades, cybersecurity was treated as a technical concern—an operational subset of information technology tasked with keeping systems running and data protected. Responsibility rested largely with IT departments, budgets were justified in terms of tools and infrastructure, and success was measured by uptime, patching cadence, and the absence of visible incidents.

That framing is now obsolete.

Modern organizations are digital by default. Core business processes, financial operations, intellectual property, service delivery, and stakeholder engagement are all mediated by technology. As a result, cybersecurity failures no longer remain contained within systems; they propagate rapidly into operational disruption, financial loss, regulatory exposure, legal liability, and reputational damage.

This shift has fundamentally altered the nature of cybersecurity. It is no longer a technical safeguard operating at the margins of the enterprise. It is a structural determinant of organizational resilience.

Yet many Boards and leadership teams continue to govern cybersecurity as if it were still a specialized IT problem. They receive briefings focused on tools deployed, vulnerabilities patched, or compliance checklists completed—without a clear understanding of how cyber risk intersects with mission execution, enterprise risk, and fiduciary responsibility.

This disconnect is not benign. It is one of the most consistent precursors to catastrophic cyber incidents.

Cybersecurity has reached a point where failure is rarely caused by a lack of technology. Instead, failure arises from gaps in oversight, unclear accountability, misaligned incentives, and the absence of disciplined governance. These are not technical shortcomings; they are leadership failures.

The purpose of this book is to articulate what cybersecurity looks like when treated correctly: as a **governance responsibility exercised by Boards and executive leadership**, supported—but not replaced—by technical expertise.

Chapter 2:

Cyber Risk as Enterprise Risk

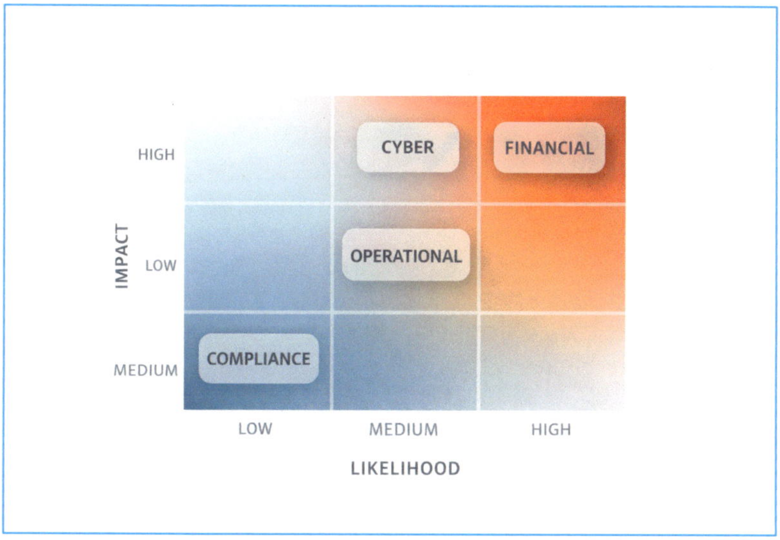

A risk heat map where: Cyber risk is plotted alongside financial, operational, compliance.

Cyber risk is enterprise risk because its consequences are enterprise-wide.

A ransomware attack may begin with a compromised endpoint, but its impact quickly extends far beyond the system that was breached. Operations halt. Revenue streams are disrupted. Sensitive data may be exposed. Regulators demand answers. Customers, donors, or partners lose confidence. Litigation risk escalates. Leadership attention is consumed for months, sometimes years.

Boards do not govern servers or networks. They govern outcomes.

When cybersecurity is framed narrowly as technical risk, it is often evaluated in isolation—detached from financial exposure, legal obligations, operational dependencies, and strategic objectives. This fragmentation obscures the true magnitude of cyber risk and leads to under-investment, misprioritization, or reactive decision-making.

By contrast, when cyber risk is treated as enterprise risk, it is governed alongside other material risks:

- financial risk,

- legal and regulatory risk,
- operational risk,
- reputational risk,
- strategic risk.

This reframing allows Boards to ask the right questions:

- What business processes would be disrupted by a cyber incident?
- What regulatory or contractual obligations would be triggered?
- What is the potential financial exposure?
- How would stakeholder trust be affected?
- How resilient is the organization's ability to recover?

These are governance questions, not technical ones.

Importantly, treating cyber risk as enterprise risk does not require Boards to become cybersecurity experts. It requires them to insist that cyber risk be translated into the same decision-making language used for other forms of risk. Impact, likelihood, consequence, and trade-offs—not tools and jargon—must drive oversight.

Cybersecurity becomes governable only when it is understood as enterprise risk.

Chapter 3: Fiduciary Duty in the Cyber Age

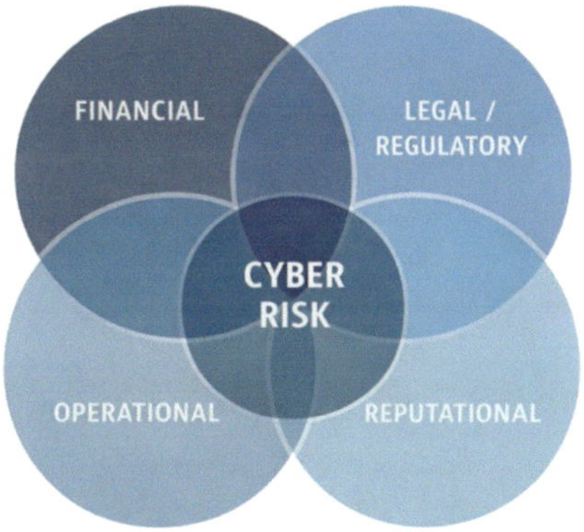

A risk convergence diagram. Four overlapping domains: Financial, Legal / Regulatory, Operational, Reputational, Cyber risk sits in the overlap, not as its own silo.

The rise of cybersecurity as a governance concern has profound implications for fiduciary duty. Directors' obligations of care, loyalty, and obedience apply fully—and increasingly visibly—to cybersecurity oversight.

The **duty of care** requires Directors to act with the level of diligence and prudence that a reasonably informed person would exercise under similar circumstances. In the cyber context, this means that Boards must take reasonable steps to understand the organization's cyber risk posture, ensure appropriate governance structures are in place, and act on material information.

Reasonable oversight does not require technical mastery. It requires informed engagement. Boards that fail to ask questions, request reporting, or respond to known deficiencies expose both the organization and themselves to significant risk.

The **duty of loyalty** requires Directors to act in the best interests of the organization. Cybersecurity decisions that defer investment, obscure risk, or prioritize short-term convenience over long-term resilience can violate this duty when they knowingly expose the organization to material harm.

The **duty of obedience** requires adherence to applicable laws, regulations, contractual obligations, and mission commitments. Cybersecurity is now embedded across these domains. Regulatory regimes increasingly mandate governance-level oversight of cyber risk. Grant agreements, contracts, and insurance policies often impose explicit cybersecurity obligations. Failure to govern cyber risk can therefore constitute a breach of legal and contractual duty.

Crucially, delegation does not eliminate fiduciary responsibility. Boards may—and should—delegate execution to management, but they retain ultimate accountability for oversight. Regulators and courts increasingly examine not whether a cyber incident occurred, but whether leadership exercised reasonable, documented, and informed oversight beforehand.

Cybersecurity governance is therefore not optional. It is a core expression of fiduciary responsibility in the digital age.

Chapter 4: Cybersecurity and Mission Failure

Cybersecurity exists to protect the organization's ability to fulfill its mission. When viewed through this lens, its relevance to governance becomes unmistakable.

For commercial enterprises, mission execution includes revenue generation, customer service, innovation, and market trust. For nonprofits and public-sector organizations, it includes service delivery, protection of vulnerable populations, stewardship of public or donor funds, and maintenance of public confidence.

Cyber incidents disrupt these outcomes directly.

A data breach that exposes sensitive information can irreparably damage trust. A ransomware attack that halts operations can prevent an organization from delivering critical services. A system outage can interrupt revenue, compliance reporting, or regulatory obligations. In each case, the impact is not merely technical—it is existential.

Boards that treat cybersecurity as a peripheral concern often do so because they fail to connect it explicitly to mission outcomes. Security investments may appear abstract or discretionary until an incident occurs. At that point, the cost of failure becomes painfully clear.

Effective governance requires Boards to reverse this logic. Cybersecurity strategy should begin with mission-critical assets and processes, not with technology inventories. Boards should ask:

- Which systems and data are essential to mission execution?
- What dependencies would cause cascading failure?

- How quickly must operations be restored to avoid unacceptable harm?
- What level of disruption is tolerable—and what is not?

When cybersecurity is aligned to mission, investment decisions become clearer, risk acceptance becomes more disciplined, and governance becomes purposeful rather than reactive.

A cyber incident that prevents an organization from fulfilling its mission is not an IT failure. It is a governance failure. Recognizing this truth is the first step toward meaningful cybersecurity governance.

Part II:

Governance Architecture for Cybersecurity

Chapter 5: Governing Versus Managing Cybersecurity

One of the most persistent failures in cybersecurity oversight arises from a fundamental category error: conflating **governance** with **management**.

Governance and management are related, but they are not interchangeable. Governance establishes direction, authority, accountability, and oversight. Management executes within that framework. When Boards attempt to manage cybersecurity directly, they often weaken both governance and execution. Conversely, when Boards disengage entirely, governance collapses into unchecked delegation.

In the cybersecurity context, this distinction is especially important because the subject matter is technical, fast-moving, and opaque to non-specialists. Directors may be tempted either to defer entirely to experts or to immerse themselves in technical detail in an attempt to compensate. Both responses are counterproductive.

To govern cybersecurity effectively, Boards must remain focused on **outcomes, structure, and accountability**, not on operational mechanics. Governing cybersecurity means ensuring that:

- clear authority exists for decision-making,
- material risks are identified and escalated,
- leadership is accountable for outcomes,
- assurance mechanisms validate effectiveness,
- decisions and deliberations are documented.

Managing cybersecurity, by contrast, involves activities such as configuring systems, deploying controls, responding to alerts, and remediating vulnerabilities.

These responsibilities properly belong to management and technical staff.

The boundary between governing and managing is not about knowledge; it is about role integrity. Boards that respect this boundary are better positioned to demand clarity, transparency, and evidence—without becoming entangled in operational detail that obscures accountability.

Effective cybersecurity governance does not require Boards to know *how* controls work. It requires them to know *that governance exists, functions as intended, and adapts to changing risk.*

Chapter 6: The Cybersecurity Governance Model

Governance without structure is aspiration. To be defensible, cybersecurity governance must be institutionalized through a clear and repeatable model.

A widely accepted approach in enterprise governance is the **three-lines-of-defense model**, adapted here specifically for cybersecurity oversight:

1. First Line – Management and Operations
Operational leadership owns cybersecurity risk. This includes system owners, business unit leaders, and technical teams responsible for implementing and operating controls. Ownership means accountability for outcomes, not merely execution of tasks.

2. Second Line – Risk and Oversight Functions

Risk management, compliance, and security governance functions define frameworks, policies, and monitoring expectations. They provide independent challenge to the first line and translate Board expectations into operational governance.

3. Third Line – Independent Assurance

Internal audit, external assessors, or independent reviewers validate whether controls are effective and whether governance mechanisms function as intended.

Boards reside above these lines. Their role is not to operate within the model, but to **ensure that the model exists, is appropriately resourced, and is functioning**.

Cybersecurity governance frequently fails when these lines are collapsed—most commonly when the same function designs controls, reports on effectiveness, and evaluates adequacy. Such arrangements create blind spots and conflicts of interest that Boards may not detect until a crisis occurs.

A defensible governance model preserves independence, enables escalation, and provides Boards with multiple perspectives on risk. It also creates resilience: when one line fails, another can detect and correct the failure before harm escalates.

Chapter 7: Roles, Responsibilities, and Authority

Ambiguity is the enemy of governance.

In cybersecurity, unclear roles and authority frequently result in unmanaged risk, delayed decisions, and ineffective incident response. When no one is clearly accountable, everyone assumes someone else is responsible.

Boards must therefore insist on explicit definition of **roles, responsibilities, and decision authority**. This is not a bureaucratic exercise; it is a governance necessity.

At a minimum, organizations should clearly articulate:

- who is accountable for cybersecurity risk at the executive level,
- who owns specific systems, data, and processes,
- who has authority to accept residual risk,
- who is responsible for escalation during incidents,
- who reports independently to the Board on risk and assurance.

It is particularly important to distinguish between **ownership** and **execution**. Technical staff may execute controls, but business leaders own the risk associated with their systems and processes. Cybersecurity risk is ultimately a business risk, not a technical one.

Similarly, the presence of a Chief Information Security Officer or equivalent does not transfer accountability away from executive leadership. Security leaders advise, design, and report—but they do not bear fiduciary responsibility for enterprise outcomes.

Boards should view role clarity as a leading indicator of governance maturity. Where authority is unclear, governance is fragile.

Chapter 8: Committees, Charters, and Reporting Discipline

Governance becomes real at the committee table.

Boards oversee cybersecurity in different ways. Some retain full-Board responsibility. Others delegate oversight to an Audit Committee, Risk Committee, or dedicated Cyber or Technology Committee. No single structure is universally correct. What matters is not the label, but the rigor of the mandate.

Effective committee-level cybersecurity governance requires:

- a clear charter defining scope and authority,
- regular, scheduled reporting,

- standardized reporting formats,
- defined escalation thresholds,
- documented deliberation and direction.

Cybersecurity oversight should not depend on ad hoc briefings or informal updates. Reporting must be structured and repeatable so that trends can be observed, risks compared over time, and decisions traced.

Boards should be cautious of cybersecurity reporting that focuses exclusively on positive achievements or technical accomplishments. Effective governance reporting includes uncomfortable information: control gaps, failed tests, unresolved risks, and emerging threats.

Documentation matters. Board minutes, briefing materials, and follow-up actions collectively form the evidentiary record of oversight. In regulatory or legal scrutiny, these artifacts often matter more than the technical details of an incident.

Cybersecurity governance should therefore be treated with the same discipline as financial oversight or legal compliance—formal, documented, and continuous.

Chapter 9: Information Flow, Escalation, and Decision Rights

Governance fails when information does not reach decision-makers in time—or reaches them stripped of context.

Boards must ensure that cybersecurity governance includes explicit rules for **information flow and escalation**. These rules define:

- what constitutes a material cyber risk,
- when management must notify executive leadership,
- when executive leadership must notify the Board,

- what information must be included in those notifications.

Escalation thresholds should be defined in advance, not improvised during crises. They should consider not only technical severity, but also potential business impact, regulatory exposure, and reputational risk.

Decision rights are equally important. During a cyber incident, time is scarce and uncertainty is high. Organizations that have not clearly defined who has authority to make key decisions—such as system shutdowns, public disclosure, or engagement with law enforcement—often lose valuable time and exacerbate harm.

Boards should not involve themselves in operational decisions during incidents. However, they must ensure that decision authority is clearly allocated and that they are informed when decisions carry material risk or consequence.

Clear information flow and decision rights transform chaos into governable action.

Chapter 10: Governance Failure Modes and Structural Warning Signs

Understanding how cybersecurity governance fails is as important as understanding how it should function.

Common governance failure modes include:

- **Over-delegation**, where Boards receive little to no substantive reporting and assume “no news is good news.”
- **Over-involvement**, where Boards immerse themselves in technical detail and obscure accountability.

- **Optimism bias**, where reporting emphasizes effort rather than effectiveness.
- **Role confusion**, where no one clearly owns risk acceptance.
- **Assurance gaps**, where control effectiveness is assumed rather than validated.

These failures rarely announce themselves directly. Instead, they appear as warning signs: inconsistent reporting, vague accountability, resistance to independent assessment, or surprise at incidents that were "unimaginable."

Boards that recognize these signals early can intervene before governance breakdown becomes organizational crisis.

Cybersecurity governance architecture is not about perfection. It is about **structural integrity**—the ability of an organization to surface risk, make decisions, and adapt under pressure.

Closing of Part II

Part I established *why* cybersecurity is a governance responsibility.
Part II establishes *how* that responsibility is institutionalized.

With governance architecture in place—roles defined, authority allocated, reporting disciplined—the organization is positioned to address the next question: **how cyber risk is evaluated and governed as a decision system**.

That is the work of Part III.

Part III:

Cyber Risk as a Board-Level System

Chapter 11: Framing Cyber Risk for Leadership Decision-Making

Risk that cannot be articulated cannot be governed.

One of the most persistent obstacles to effective cybersecurity governance is the way cyber risk is communicated to Boards and executive leadership. Too often, reporting is dominated by technical language, control inventories, or vulnerability counts that provide activity visibility but obscure decision relevance.

Boards do not govern systems. They govern exposure, consequence, and trade-offs.

Effective cyber risk framing translates technical realities into **decision-grade information**. This translation is not dilution; it is discipline. Cyber risk must be expressed in terms that allow leadership to weigh it alongside financial, legal, operational, and strategic risks.

At a governance level, cyber risk should always be framed through four questions:

1. What could happen?

This includes plausible threat scenarios, not abstract possibilities.

2. How likely is it?

Likelihood need not be precise, but it must be reasoned and comparative.

3. What would the impact be?

Impact should be expressed in mission, financial, regulatory, and reputational terms.

4. What are our options?

Mitigation, transfer, avoidance, or acceptance—each with trade-offs.

When cyber risk is framed this way, Boards are able to engage productively without needing to master technical detail. Conversely, when reporting focuses on vulnerabilities patched or tools deployed, Boards are left without a basis for judgment.

Governance requires translation. Without it, cybersecurity remains opaque and ungovernable.

Chapter 12:

Risk Appetite, Tolerance, and the Limits of Security

Every organization accepts risk. The only question is whether that acceptance is **intentional or accidental**.

Risk appetite defines how much risk an organization is willing to tolerate in pursuit of its objectives. In cybersecurity, risk appetite is often implicit, unexamined, or assumed to be "as little risk as possible." This assumption is neither realistic nor governable.

Perfect security does not exist. Attempting to eliminate all cyber risk is neither feasible nor economically rational. Boards must therefore confront the uncomfortable but necessary task of defining **what**

levels of cyber risk are acceptable—and which are not.

A meaningful cyber risk appetite statement addresses:

- unacceptable outcomes (e.g., prolonged mission interruption, regulatory violation, exposure of highly sensitive data),
- tolerable levels of disruption or loss,
- conditions under which risk may be accepted,
- authority required for risk acceptance decisions.

Risk tolerance is not static. It may vary by asset, process, or context. A Board may tolerate limited disruption to non-critical systems but have zero tolerance for compromise of regulated data or life-critical operations.

Importantly, risk appetite does not authorize negligence. Accepting risk does not mean ignoring it. It means recognizing residual exposure after reasonable mitigation and making a deliberate decision to proceed.

Boards that fail to articulate risk appetite often discover—too late—that they have been accepting risks they would never have approved explicitly.

Chapter 13: Enterprise Cyber Risk Assessment as a Governance Tool

Risk assessment is frequently misunderstood as a compliance artifact rather than a governance instrument. When treated as a checklist exercise, it produces volume without insight. When governed properly, it becomes one of the most powerful decision-support tools available to leadership.

At the Board level, the purpose of cyber risk assessment is not to catalog every vulnerability. It is to identify **where the organization is most exposed to material harm**.

Effective enterprise cyber risk assessments share several characteristics:

They focus on **business processes and mission-critical functions**, not merely on technology assets. They consider how systems support operations, revenue, compliance, and service delivery.

They evaluate **threat scenarios**, not just control gaps. This includes external threats, insider risk, third-party compromise, and systemic failures.

They incorporate **third-party and supply-chain dependencies**, recognizing that risk increasingly originates outside organizational boundaries.

They explicitly consider **regulatory and contractual consequences**, not just technical impact.

Boards should expect risk assessments to inform priorities, guide investment decisions, and shape oversight focus. Assessments that do not influence strategy or resource allocation are governance failures, regardless of how comprehensive they appear.

Risk assessment is not an end in itself. It is a means of enabling informed leadership judgment.

Chapter 14: Risk Treatment, Acceptance, and Governance Discipline

Risk governance culminates in decisions.

Once risks are identified and assessed, leadership must determine how to respond. The available options—mitigation, transfer, avoidance, or acceptance—are well known. What distinguishes strong governance is **how deliberately those options are exercised**.

Mitigation involves implementing controls to reduce likelihood or impact. Transfer may include insurance or contractual risk sharing. Avoidance may require discontinuing activities or redesigning processes.

Acceptance acknowledges residual risk after reasonable mitigation.

Boards play a critical role in ensuring that risk acceptance is **explicit, documented, and revisited**. Silence or inertia must never be treated as implicit acceptance.

High-impact or material cyber risks should require formal acceptance at the executive level, with Board awareness or approval depending on severity. Documentation of acceptance decisions is essential—not to assign blame, but to demonstrate informed judgment.

Cyber insurance deserves special attention. Insurance can mitigate financial impact, but it does not reduce operational disruption, reputational damage, or regulatory scrutiny. Boards should be wary of treating insurance as a substitute for governance or control.

Risk treatment decisions are expressions of organizational values and priorities. Governing them requires discipline, not optimism.

Chapter 15: Cybersecurity Investment as Risk Governance

Cybersecurity spending is often reactive, driven by incidents, audits, or vendor persuasion. This approach leads to tool proliferation, inconsistent coverage, and unclear return on investment.

Boards govern capital allocation. Cybersecurity investment should be subject to the same scrutiny as any other material expenditure.

Effective governance requires that cybersecurity investments be evaluated in terms of **risk reduction and mission protection**, not feature sets or marketing claims. Boards should expect management to articulate:

- which risks the investment addresses,

- how it reduces likelihood or impact,
- what residual risk remains,
- how effectiveness will be measured.

Spending more does not necessarily mean being safer. Many organizations with significant cybersecurity budgets remain highly vulnerable due to misaligned priorities or weak governance.

Conversely, disciplined investment aligned to risk assessment can materially improve resilience without excessive cost.

Cybersecurity investment is not about buying security. It is about **governing exposure**.

Chapter 16: Risk Ownership, Accountability, and Escalation

Cyber risk does not belong to the security function alone. It belongs to the business.

One of the most damaging governance myths is that cybersecurity risk is owned by technical teams. In reality, risk ownership resides with those who own the business processes, data, and outcomes affected by cyber events.

Boards should require clear designation of risk owners for major systems and processes. These owners are accountable for understanding risk, supporting mitigation, and escalating issues when risk exceeds tolerance.

Escalation is a governance function, not a failure. Organizations that punish escalation or reward silence create conditions in which risks remain hidden until they become crises.

Clear escalation thresholds—based on impact, not embarrassment—enable timely leadership intervention. Boards should ensure that escalation paths are formalized, protected, and exercised.

Risk governance fails when accountability is diffuse. It succeeds when ownership is clear and supported by authority.

Closing of Part III

With Parts I through III, the foundation of cybersecurity governance is established:

- **Part I** defined cybersecurity as a governance obligation.
- **Part II** institutionalized oversight through governance architecture.
- **Part III** transformed cybersecurity into a **Board-level risk system** capable of informed decision-making.

The next challenge is ensuring that governance intent becomes enforceable reality. That transition occurs through **policy**—the subject of Part IV.

Part IV:

Policy as a Governance Instrument

Chapter 17: Policy as an Instrument of Governance, Not Administration

In many organizations, policy is treated as administrative overhead: a collection of documents produced to satisfy auditors, insurers, or regulators, then filed away and rarely revisited. This perception is both common and deeply flawed.

Policy is not an operational artifact. It is a **governance instrument**.

At its core, policy performs three essential governance functions. First, it establishes **authority**—who is empowered to make decisions and enforce requirements. Second, it defines **expectations**—what behaviors, controls, and outcomes are required. Third, it creates **accountability**—a standard against which actions can be evaluated.

From a Board perspective, policy is one of the few durable mechanisms through which intent is translated into organizational obligation. Unlike strategy statements or management presentations, policy carries formal weight. It can be adopted, enforced, audited, cited, and relied upon as evidence of governance.

In the cybersecurity context, policy is especially critical because of the technical complexity and distributed nature of risk. Without clear policy direction, cybersecurity efforts often devolve into inconsistent practices driven by local priorities rather than enterprise risk considerations.

Boards that fail to treat cybersecurity policy as a governance tool often discover—during regulatory examination or litigation—that they lack clear evidence of expectations, authority, or oversight. Conversely, Boards that adopt, review, and enforce cybersecurity policy create a defensible governance record even when incidents occur.

Policy does not prevent every failure. It ensures that failures are governed.

Chapter 18: Policy Hierarchy, Authority, and Board Ownership

Not all policies are equal, and not all policies belong at the same level of governance.

Effective cybersecurity governance depends on a **clear policy hierarchy** that aligns authority with responsibility. At the top of this hierarchy sit **Board-level policies**. These establish the existence of the cybersecurity program, articulate organizational objectives, and delegate authority to executive leadership.

Below these sit **executive and management policies**, which operationalize Board intent. Standards, procedures, and technical guidelines then implement controls in practice.

When this hierarchy is unclear, governance erodes. Technical policies may proliferate without strategic alignment, while Boards remain disconnected from the substance of cybersecurity governance. Alternatively, Boards may be asked to approve overly detailed documents that obscure accountability and dilute oversight.

Boards should therefore limit their direct policy approval to a **small number of governance-level cybersecurity policies**, typically including:

- an overarching cybersecurity or information security policy,
- a risk management or risk appetite policy,
- an incident response governance policy,
- a third-party or vendor risk governance policy,
- a data protection and classification policy.

Ownership matters. Policies adopted by the Board carry institutional authority and signal organizational priority. They also create a clear record of oversight, particularly when accompanied by formal review and re-adoption cycles.

Delegation of policy implementation does not diminish Board ownership of policy intent. Boards govern by setting expectations and requiring evidence that those expectations are met.

Chapter 19: Core Cybersecurity Governance Policies

While the specific content of cybersecurity policies will vary by organization and sector, effective governance requires coverage of several core domains. These policies form the backbone of cybersecurity governance and are frequently scrutinized by regulators, auditors, and courts.

An **Information Security Policy** establishes baseline expectations for protecting the confidentiality, integrity, and availability of information and systems. It defines scope, applicability, and accountability, making clear that cybersecurity is an organizational responsibility rather than a technical specialty.

A **Cyber Risk Management Policy** defines how cybersecurity risk is identified, assessed, treated, and monitored. It connects cybersecurity explicitly to enterprise risk management and clarifies authority for risk acceptance.

An **Incident Response and Breach Governance Policy** defines leadership roles, escalation thresholds, decision authority, and notification obligations during cyber incidents. This policy is particularly critical because it governs behavior under pressure, when improvisation often leads to error.

A **Third-Party and Vendor Risk Policy** extends governance beyond organizational boundaries. It establishes expectations for due diligence, contractual controls, monitoring, and exit planning, recognizing that modern cyber risk frequently originates within the supply chain.

A **Data Classification and Protection Policy** governs how information is categorized, handled, retained, and disposed of. It is essential for aligning cybersecurity with privacy, regulatory compliance, and ethical stewardship.

Boards need not draft these policies, but they must understand their purpose, approve them at the appropriate level, and require evidence of enforcement.

Chapter 20: Policy as Evidence of Due Diligence

Policy occupies a unique position in governance because it functions simultaneously as instruction and evidence.

In regulatory investigations, audits, and litigation, policy documents are often among the first artifacts requested. They answer foundational questions:

- What did the organization say it would do?
- Who was responsible?
- Were expectations reasonable?
- Were they communicated and enforced?

Well-crafted policies demonstrate that leadership understood its obligations and took reasonable steps to address them. Poorly drafted or outdated policies can have the opposite effect, creating a record of neglect or misalignment.

Boards should therefore treat policy quality as a governance concern. Vague language, undefined roles, and unenforceable requirements weaken governance rather than strengthen it.

Equally important is the relationship between policy and practice. Policies that are ignored, unknown, or routinely violated undermine credibility. Boards should require management to demonstrate not only that policies exist, but that they are communicated, understood, and enforced.

Policy is not proof of effectiveness, but it is proof of intent. In governance, intent matters.

Chapter 21: Policy Lifecycle Management and Governance Drift

Cybersecurity policy cannot be static. The threat landscape evolves, technologies change, regulatory expectations expand, and organizational structures shift. Policies that fail to evolve with these changes become liabilities.

Governance drift occurs when policies no longer reflect reality, yet remain formally in force. This drift creates a dangerous gap between documented expectations and actual practice. During scrutiny, this gap is often interpreted as governance failure.

Boards should therefore require a formal **policy lifecycle**, including:

- defined review cycles,
- triggers for out-of-cycle updates,
- version control and change documentation,
- formal re-approval where appropriate.

Annual review is a common baseline, but review should also be triggered by material incidents, significant organizational changes, or major regulatory developments.

Importantly, policy review should be substantive, not perfunctory. Boards should expect management to identify whether policies remain fit for purpose, not merely confirm their existence.

Policy lifecycle management is not administrative housekeeping. It is an essential component of credible governance.

Chapter 22: Exceptions, Enforcement, and Governance Integrity

No policy regime is absolute. Exceptions will occur. What distinguishes strong governance from weak governance is **how exceptions are handled**.

Uncontrolled exceptions erode governance by creating informal norms that supersede policy. Controlled exceptions, by contrast, reinforce governance by demonstrating discipline and accountability.

Boards should require that:

- policy exceptions be formally documented,
- exceptions include rationale, scope, and duration,

- approval authority be clearly defined,
- exceptions be reviewed and renewed or retired.

Enforcement is equally important. Policies without enforcement are suggestions, not governance instruments. Boards should expect clear consequences for non-compliance, applied consistently and proportionately.

Governance integrity depends on credibility. When employees observe that policies are selectively enforced or routinely ignored, trust in leadership erodes and risk increases.

Policy, when governed properly, becomes a stabilizing force—providing clarity, consistency, and accountability even under pressure.

Closing of Part IV

Policy is where governance becomes tangible.

With Parts I through IV, the organization has:

- recognized cybersecurity as a governance obligation,
- established governance architecture,
- framed cyber risk as a decision system,
- translated intent into enforceable policy.

Part V addresses the question every Board eventually faces—often under uncomfortable circumstances:

“How do we actually know this is working?”

The question is whether governance mechanisms actually work in practice. That question can only be answered through **assurance, oversight, and continuous monitoring**—the focus of Part V.

Part V is about **proof, validation, and disciplined skepticism**. It is where governance stops being aspirational and becomes **defensible.**

Part V:

Assurance, Oversight, and Continuous Monitoring

Chapter 23: Assurance Versus Activity: Knowing the Difference

One of the most common failures in cybersecurity governance is mistaking **activity** for **assurance**.

Organizations are often very busy with cybersecurity. Systems are patched, tools are deployed, alerts are investigated, training is conducted, and reports are generated. These activities may be necessary, but they do not answer the question Boards must ask:

Are our controls effective?

Activity describes what was done. Assurance evaluates whether what was done actually reduces risk.

Boards frequently receive cybersecurity briefings that emphasize volume—numbers of vulnerabilities remediated, systems scanned, employees trained. While such information can demonstrate effort, it provides little insight into whether the organization is meaningfully protected against material risk.

Assurance, by contrast, is outcome-oriented. It asks whether controls function as intended, whether governance mechanisms operate reliably, and whether leadership would know if something were failing.

This distinction is critical because governance collapses when Boards assume that effort equals effectiveness. Many organizations that suffer major cyber incidents were demonstrably "doing cybersecurity" beforehand. What they lacked was assurance.

Effective cybersecurity governance therefore requires Boards to demand **independent validation**, not just management reporting.

Chapter 24: Independent Validation and the Role of Assurance Functions

Assurance gains credibility when it is independent of execution.

In cybersecurity governance, independence does not necessarily mean external auditors alone, though they can play an important role. Independence means that the function evaluating effectiveness is not the same function responsible for implementing controls.

Internal audit, risk assurance teams, third-party assessors, and external auditors all contribute to this validation ecosystem. Each provides a different lens on governance and control effectiveness.

Boards should expect assurance activities to address questions such as:

- Are cybersecurity controls designed appropriately?
- Are they implemented consistently?
- Do they operate effectively over time?
- Are exceptions identified, tracked, and resolved?
- Does management respond appropriately to findings?

Importantly, assurance should extend beyond technical controls. Governance structures, escalation mechanisms, incident response processes, and Board reporting pathways should all be subject to validation.

Assurance that focuses only on technology while ignoring governance is incomplete. Boards govern systems of accountability, not just systems of software.

Chapter 25: Management Review, Internal Audit, and Board Oversight

Assurance does not replace oversight. It informs it.

Boards should require regular management review of cybersecurity governance and control effectiveness. These reviews should be structured, documented, and focused on risk rather than compliance formalities.

Internal audit plays a particularly important role in this process. When properly scoped, internal audit provides Boards with an independent assessment of whether cybersecurity governance mechanisms are functioning as intended.

However, internal audit effectiveness depends on mandate and independence. Boards should ensure that audit plans include cybersecurity governance—not just IT controls—and that auditors have sufficient authority and expertise to challenge management assumptions.

Board oversight completes the loop. Assurance findings that are not reviewed, discussed, and acted upon by the Board lose their governance value. Boards should expect management to present not only findings, but remediation plans and timelines.

Governance is iterative. Assurance informs oversight, oversight drives action, and action is reassessed through assurance.

Chapter 26: Metrics That Inform Governance, Not Noise

Metrics are essential to oversight, but only when they are carefully chosen.

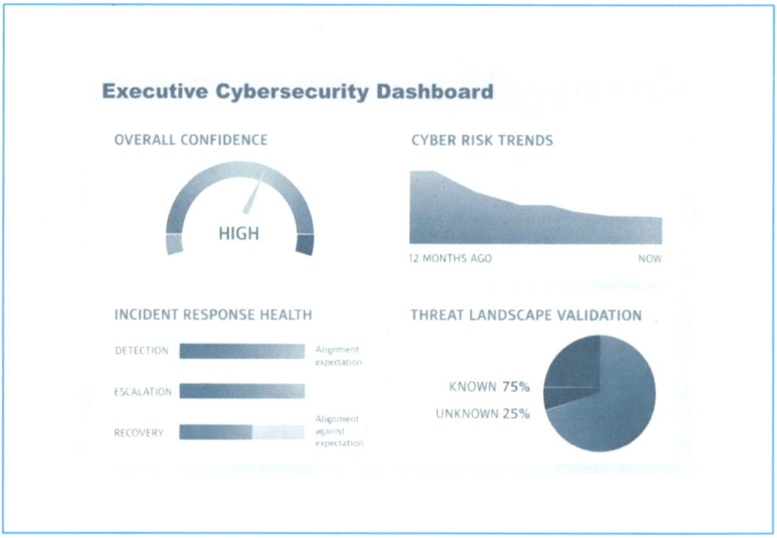

Mock executive dashboard. Confidence indicators, not technical stats. Trends, not alerts. Entirely fictional, but realistic.

One of the most persistent frustrations for Boards is receiving cybersecurity metrics that are either too technical to interpret or too superficial to be useful. Dashboards filled with red, yellow, and green indicators may look authoritative while obscuring substantive risk.

Governance-grade cybersecurity metrics share several characteristics.

They are **decision-relevant**. Each metric should inform a question the Board is expected to consider, such as whether risk is increasing, whether controls are degrading, or whether investment is yielding benefit.

They emphasize **trends over snapshots**. A single data point rarely conveys governance insight. Trends reveal whether the organization is improving, stagnating, or deteriorating.

They align with **risk and impact**, not effort. Counting actions taken is less useful than understanding exposure reduced or resilience gained.

They include **leading and lagging indicators**. Lagging indicators show what has already happened. Leading indicators suggest where problems may emerge.

Boards should also be wary of metric saturation. More data does not equal better governance. Discipline lies in selecting a small number of meaningful indicators and insisting on consistent reporting.

Metrics do not govern. Boards do. Metrics exist to support judgment, not replace it.

Chapter 27: Continuous Monitoring as a Governance Feedback Loop

Cybersecurity governance cannot be static because risk is not static.

Continuous monitoring—of systems, controls, threats, and governance processes—provides the feedback necessary to adapt oversight and strategy over time. From a Board perspective, continuous monitoring is not about real-time dashboards. It is about **early warning**.

Boards should expect governance systems that surface:

- emerging risk trends,
- degradation in control effectiveness,

- changes in threat landscape,
- impacts of organizational change (such as growth, mergers, or technology adoption).

This information should feed back into risk assessment, investment prioritization, and policy review. When monitoring reveals deterioration or emerging exposure, governance must respond.

Organizations that treat monitoring as an operational activity disconnected from governance often fail to adapt until an incident forces attention. Continuous monitoring closes the loop between intent and reality.

Chapter 28: Escalation, Transparency, and the Courage to Surface Bad News

Governance fails not when bad things happen, but when bad news is suppressed.

One of the most dangerous dynamics in cybersecurity governance is the silent normalization of risk. Control gaps are rationalized. Delays are minimized. Findings are reframed. Over time, leadership develops a false sense of security.

Boards must therefore actively cultivate an environment where escalation is expected and protected. Assurance findings, negative trends, and unresolved risks must be surfaced without fear of reprisal.

Transparency is not a cultural nicety; it is a governance requirement. Organizations that punish messengers or reward optimism create blind spots that no amount of technology can overcome.

Boards set the tone. When Directors respond constructively to uncomfortable information—asking questions, allocating resources, and supporting remediation—they reinforce governance integrity. When they react defensively or dismissively, risk goes underground.

Effective oversight requires disciplined skepticism paired with trust in process.

Closing of Part V

With Part V, cybersecurity governance acquires its most critical attribute: **credibility**.

Policies, frameworks, and reporting mean little unless they are tested, validated, and challenged. Assurance, oversight, and continuous monitoring provide the evidence that governance functions as intended—or the warning that it does not.

At this stage in the framework:

- authority has been established,
- risk has been framed,
- policy has been codified,
- effectiveness is now being evaluated.

The remaining challenge is leadership under pressure—**how governance performs when incidents occur**. That challenge is addressed in Part VI.

Part VI:

Incident Preparedness and Leadership Decision-Making

Chapter 29: Cyber Incidents as Organizational Crises

Cyber incidents are not technical events. They are organizational crises.

While an incident may begin with a compromised system or malicious code, its defining characteristics quickly transcend technology. Time pressure, incomplete information, legal exposure, regulatory obligations, reputational risk, and intense external scrutiny converge simultaneously. Decisions made in hours—or even minutes—can have consequences that persist for years.

Organizations that approach cyber incidents as technical problems to be "fixed" often lose control of the narrative, the timeline, and the outcome. Those that treat incidents as governance events—requiring leadership judgment, authority, and coordination—are far more likely to preserve trust and limit harm.

From a Board perspective, the question is not whether management can remediate malware. It is whether leadership can:

- make defensible decisions with imperfect information,
- balance competing obligations,
- communicate responsibly with stakeholders,
- preserve evidence and governance credibility.

Cyber incidents expose the difference between **operational readiness** and **governance readiness**. The former focuses on tools and procedures. The latter focuses on authority, escalation, and judgment.

This chapter establishes a critical premise for Boards:

incident response is a leadership function, not an IT exercise.

Chapter 30: Preparedness as a Governance Responsibility

Preparedness does not begin when an incident occurs. It begins long before, through deliberate governance design.

Boards often assume that preparedness resides within technical incident response plans. While such plans are necessary, they are insufficient. True preparedness encompasses leadership roles, decision rights, communication protocols, and legal considerations.

Governance-level preparedness requires clarity on several questions:

- Who has authority to declare an incident?
- Who decides whether systems are shut down?
- Who determines regulatory notification obligations?
- Who approves external communications?
- When and how is the Board notified?

Absent predefined answers, organizations improvise under stress. Improvisation during crises often leads to delay, inconsistency, and error.

Boards should ensure that preparedness is addressed through formal governance artifacts, including incident response governance policies, executive playbooks, and escalation protocols. These instruments do not remove uncertainty, but they provide structure when uncertainty is unavoidable.

Preparedness is not about predicting every scenario. It is about ensuring that leadership knows **how to govern when prediction fails**.

Chapter 31: Executive Authority, Escalation, and Decision Rights During Incidents

Cyber incidents compress time and amplify ambiguity. In this environment, unclear authority becomes a critical vulnerability.

Effective governance requires that decision rights during incidents be explicitly defined and widely understood. This includes authority over:

- operational containment actions,
- engagement with external experts or law enforcement,
- regulatory notification and disclosure,
- public and stakeholder communications.

Boards should not insert themselves into operational decision-making during live incidents. However, they must ensure that authority is properly allocated and that escalation thresholds are clear.

Escalation is not a signal of failure; it is a signal of governance functioning as intended. Organizations that delay escalation out of fear, embarrassment, or uncertainty often worsen outcomes.

Boards should expect incident escalation criteria to be based on **potential impact**, not technical severity alone. An incident with limited technical scope may still carry material regulatory or reputational consequences.

Clear authority and disciplined escalation transform crisis response from chaos into governable action.

Chapter 32:
The Board's Role During a Cyber Incident

Boards do not manage incidents, but they do govern them.

The Board's role during a cyber incident is to:

- receive timely, accurate information,
- exercise oversight of leadership decisions,
- ensure that legal and fiduciary obligations are met,
- support management without undermining authority,
- document deliberation and direction.

Boards should not attempt to direct technical response or substitute judgment for management. Such involvement blurs accountability and can interfere with response efforts.

Instead, Boards should focus on:

- understanding the nature and potential impact of the incident,
- confirming that appropriate expertise is engaged,
- ensuring regulatory and disclosure obligations are considered,
- verifying that communications align with organizational values and obligations.

Documentation is critical. Board briefings, questions, and guidance during incidents form part of the governance record. This record may later be scrutinized by regulators, litigators, or insurers.

Effective Board conduct during incidents balances engagement with restraint—active oversight without operational interference.

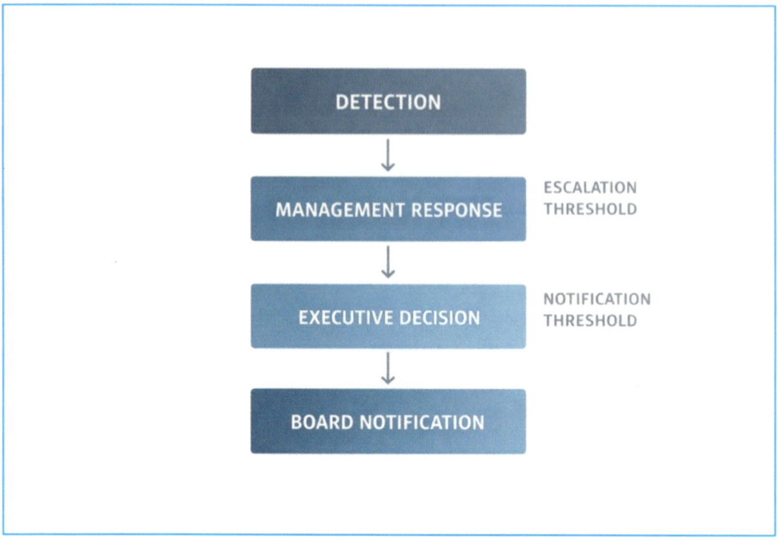

A vertical escalation flow: Detection, Management response, Executive decision, Board notification, Clear thresholds, not timelines.

Chapter 33:

Legal, Regulatory, and Disclosure Considerations

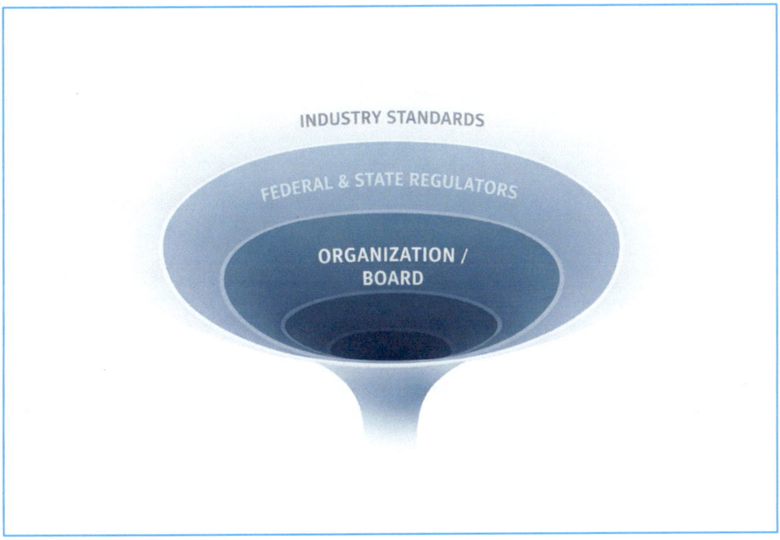

A gravity-well style diagram:, Outer rings: Industry standards, Inner rings: Federal and state regulators, Center: Organization / Board

Cyber incidents are legal events as much as technical ones.

Regulatory regimes increasingly impose strict notification and disclosure requirements tied to cybersecurity incidents. Contractual obligations, grant conditions, and insurance policies often impose additional requirements.

Boards must ensure that incident governance integrates legal counsel early and continuously. Decisions regarding notification, disclosure, and communication should be informed by legal analysis, not reactive impulse.

Timing is especially critical. Delayed or incomplete disclosures can trigger regulatory penalties and undermine credibility. Premature or inaccurate disclosures can create unnecessary exposure.

Boards should expect leadership to balance transparency with accuracy, recognizing that facts often evolve during incidents. Governance structures must support careful, principled decision-making under these conditions.

Legal and regulatory obligations do not eliminate discretion, but they narrow it. Boards must ensure that leadership understands where discretion exists—and where it does not.

Chapter 34: Tabletop Exercises as Governance Validation

Tabletop exercises are often misunderstood as training simulations. In governance terms, they are **stress tests**.

Well-designed tabletop exercises evaluate whether governance structures function under pressure. They test escalation pathways, decision authority, communication protocols, and Board-management interaction.

Boards should participate directly in periodic tabletop exercises focused on:

- executive-level decision-making,
- regulatory and disclosure dilemmas,
- reputational and stakeholder impacts,

- cross-functional coordination.

The value of tabletop exercises lies not in performance perfection, but in exposure of gaps. Exercises that do not reveal discomfort or uncertainty are likely insufficiently realistic.

Critically, tabletop exercises must produce governance outcomes: documented findings, assigned remediation, and follow-up. Exercises without consequence are theater.

Boards that engage seriously in tabletop exercises demonstrate a level of preparedness that cannot be replicated through policy alone.

Chapter 35: Post-Incident Review and Governance Learning

Governance responsibility does not end when an incident is resolved.

Post-incident review is essential to restoring trust, improving resilience, and demonstrating accountability. Boards should require structured reviews that examine not only technical root causes, but also governance performance.

Effective post-incident reviews address questions such as:

- Were escalation and notification timely?
- Were decision rights clear and exercised appropriately?

- Did governance structures support or hinder response?
- Were communications accurate and aligned with obligations?
- What governance changes are required to reduce future risk?

The purpose of review is not blame. It is learning. Organizations that treat incidents as failures to be hidden miss the opportunity to strengthen governance.

Boards play a critical role in ensuring that lessons learned translate into concrete action—policy updates, structural changes, investment decisions, and training enhancements.

Crisis, when governed well, becomes a catalyst for maturity.

Closing of Part VI

Cyber incidents test governance more severely than any audit or assessment. They reveal whether authority is clear, whether leadership is prepared, and whether Boards can exercise oversight under pressure.

With Part VI, the framework has now addressed:

- recognition of cybersecurity as a governance obligation,
- establishment of governance architecture,
- framing of cyber risk as a decision system,
- codification through policy,
- validation through assurance,
- and leadership conduct during crisis.

The remaining challenge is broader still: cybersecurity does not stop at organizational boundaries. **Third-party dependencies, ecosystems, culture, and long-term resilience** remain to be governed.

That work begins in Part VII.

PART VII:

THIRD-PARTY, VENDOR, AND ECOSYSTEM RISK

Chapter 36: The Myth of the Organizational Boundary

Traditional governance models assume that risk is largely internal: systems owned, staff employed, controls operated directly by the organization. That assumption is no longer valid.

Modern organizations operate within dense digital ecosystems. Cloud providers host critical systems. Software vendors process sensitive data. Managed service providers administer infrastructure. Partners exchange information continuously. In many cases, third parties now have more access to organizational data and systems than internal staff.

From a cybersecurity perspective, the organizational boundary has dissolved.

Yet governance has not always kept pace with this reality. Boards may govern internal controls rigorously while treating third-party risk as a procurement or IT concern. This disconnect creates one of the most significant and least visible sources of cyber exposure.

Cyber incidents originating through third parties are rarely viewed as excusable. Regulators, courts, and stakeholders increasingly hold organizations responsible for the risks they choose to inherit through outsourcing, integration, and partnership.

The central governance question is therefore not *"Did the vendor cause the problem?"* but *"Did the organization govern its dependencies responsibly?"*

Chapter 37: Extended Enterprise Risk as a Governance Concern

Third-party cyber risk is not simply a subset of operational risk. It is a distinct governance challenge because control and accountability are distributed across organizational boundaries.

Boards must recognize that:

- vendor security failures can have enterprise-level consequences,
- contractual relationships do not transfer fiduciary responsibility,
- visibility into third-party controls is often limited,
- dependency concentration can amplify impact.

Extended enterprise risk includes not only direct vendors, but also subcontractors, cloud service providers, software supply chains, and data-sharing partners. In complex ecosystems, risk propagation may occur several layers removed from the original contractual relationship.

Effective governance requires Boards to elevate third-party cyber risk from an operational checklist to a **standing oversight concern**. This includes understanding where the organization is most dependent on external parties for mission-critical functions and where single points of failure exist.

Ignoring extended enterprise risk does not eliminate it. It merely renders it invisible until failure occurs.

Chapter 38: Due Diligence Beyond the Checkbox

Vendor due diligence is often treated as a one-time compliance exercise performed during procurement. Questionnaires are completed, certifications are collected, and contracts are signed. Governance attention then shifts elsewhere.

This approach is inadequate.

Due diligence is not about form completion; it is about **risk-informed decision-making**. Boards should expect that vendor due diligence addresses:

- the criticality of the service or data involved,

- the vendor's security governance and maturity,
- regulatory and legal exposure created by the relationship,
- dependency and concentration risk,
- exit feasibility and transition risk.

Not all vendors require the same level of scrutiny. Governance discipline lies in aligning due diligence depth to potential impact. Over-scrutinizing low-risk vendors wastes resources, while under-scrutinizing critical vendors creates existential exposure.

Boards need not review individual vendor assessments, but they must ensure that a **risk-based due diligence framework exists and is enforced**.

Chapter 39: Contractual Controls and the Limits of Paper Governance

Contracts are an essential governance tool—but they are not controls.

Security clauses, audit rights, notification requirements, and indemnification provisions establish expectations and remedies. They do not, by themselves, reduce risk.

Boards should be cautious of governance approaches that rely primarily on contractual language as a substitute for oversight. A contract that is never enforced, audited, or revisited provides false comfort.

Effective third-party governance requires:

- clear security expectations embedded in contracts,
- defined incident notification timelines,
- rights to audit or obtain assurance,
- consequences for non-compliance,
- alignment between contractual obligations and actual practice.

Importantly, contractual governance must be coordinated across legal, procurement, risk, and security functions. Fragmented ownership leads to gaps where no one is responsible for ensuring that contractual protections are meaningful.

Contracts define the rules of engagement. Governance determines whether those rules matter.

Chapter 40: Ongoing Monitoring and the Illusion of Static Risk

Third-party risk does not remain constant over time.

Vendors change ownership, financial condition, technology stacks, and security posture. Threat landscapes evolve. Regulatory expectations shift. What was acceptable risk at onboarding may become unacceptable years later.

Boards must therefore ensure that third-party cyber risk governance includes **ongoing monitoring**, not just initial vetting. This may include periodic reassessment, review of assurance reports, monitoring of incidents, and evaluation of emerging dependency risks.

Static risk models fail in dynamic ecosystems. Governance that assumes yesterday's assessment applies indefinitely invites surprise.

Monitoring does not require constant surveillance of every vendor. It requires targeted attention to vendors whose failure would cause disproportionate harm.

Boards should expect management to articulate how ongoing third-party risk is monitored, escalated, and addressed.

Chapter 41: Concentration, Dependency, and Exit Risk

One of the most underappreciated dimensions of third-party cyber risk is **dependency concentration**.

Organizations often consolidate services for efficiency, cost, or convenience. Cloud providers, managed service platforms, and software ecosystems promise scale and simplicity. In doing so, they also create single points of failure.

Boards should ask:

- Which vendors, if unavailable or compromised, would halt mission-critical operations?
- How quickly could the organization transition to an alternative?
- Are exit plans realistic, tested, and resourced?

Exit risk is a governance concern, not an operational inconvenience. An organization that cannot disengage from a failing or compromised vendor is effectively captive to that risk.

Boards need not demand immediate redundancy for every service, but they should insist that dependency risks are understood, documented, and deliberately accepted where unavoidable.

Chapter 42: Accountability for Third-Party Risk Governance

A common governance failure occurs when third-party risk is treated as "everyone's responsibility"—which in practice means no one's responsibility.

Effective governance requires clear accountability for:

- third-party risk frameworks,
- due diligence execution,
- contract security alignment,
- ongoing monitoring,
- incident coordination with vendors.

Boards should ensure that executive ownership of third-party cyber risk is explicit and that reporting on extended enterprise risk is integrated into regular cybersecurity oversight.

When third-party incidents occur, regulators and stakeholders rarely accept “the vendor failed” as a sufficient explanation. They look instead at whether the organization governed its dependencies responsibly.

Accountability cannot be outsourced.

Closing of Part VII

Cybersecurity governance cannot stop at the edge of the organization.

With Part VII, the framework acknowledges a critical reality of modern enterprises: **risk is increasingly inherited through ecosystems rather than generated internally**. Governing that risk requires discipline, clarity, and sustained oversight.

At this stage, the framework has addressed:

- governance responsibility,
- internal architecture,
- risk decision systems,
- policy authority,
- assurance and validation,
- crisis leadership,
- and extended enterprise exposure.

What remains is the human dimension: culture, ethics, trust, and long-term resilience. These elements determine whether governance frameworks endure—or quietly erode.

That work begins in Part VIII.

Part VIII:

Culture, Ethics, and Organizational Resilience

Chapter 43: Cybersecurity Culture as a Board Responsibility

Organizational culture is not created by policy alone. It is created by what leadership consistently rewards, tolerates, and enforces.

Cybersecurity culture, in particular, reflects how an organization understands responsibility, accountability, and risk. When cybersecurity is treated as a technical inconvenience or a compliance obligation, employees behave accordingly. When it is treated as a shared responsibility tied to mission and values, behavior changes.

Boards play a decisive role in shaping this culture, whether intentionally or not. The questions Directors ask, the issues they prioritize, and the consequences they support all signal what truly matters.

A Board that engages cybersecurity only after an incident sends a clear message: security is secondary until failure forces attention. A Board that asks disciplined questions, demands evidence, and supports remediation communicates that cybersecurity is integral to responsible leadership.

Cybersecurity culture is therefore not a grassroots phenomenon. It is a **governance outcome**.

Chapter 44: Tone at the Top and Behavioral Signals

"Tone at the top" is often invoked as an abstract governance principle. In cybersecurity, it manifests in concrete and observable ways.

Boards influence tone through:

- the seriousness with which cyber risk is discussed,
- the willingness to fund risk-aligned investments,
- the response to bad news and assurance findings,
- the consistency of enforcement when policies are violated.

Employees and managers quickly learn whether cybersecurity expectations are aspirational or enforceable. If leadership minimizes findings, delays remediation, or penalizes escalation, a culture of silence and risk normalization emerges.

Conversely, when Boards respond constructively to uncomfortable information—acknowledging risk, allocating resources, and supporting accountability—they reinforce a culture of transparency and resilience.

Tone at the top is not what Boards say in policy statements. It is what the organization observes when trade-offs are made under pressure.

Chapter 45:

Ethics, Data Stewardship, and Moral Obligation

Cybersecurity governance is inseparable from ethics.

Organizations increasingly hold vast amounts of sensitive information: personal data, financial records, intellectual property, proprietary research, and confidential communications. Legal compliance defines minimum requirements, but ethical stewardship often demands more.

Boards must grapple with questions that extend beyond regulation:

- What obligations do we owe to individuals whose data we hold?

- How do we balance operational convenience against privacy?
- How transparent should we be when harm occurs?
- How do our cybersecurity practices align with our stated values?

Ethical governance recognizes that data subjects are not abstractions. Breaches affect real people—sometimes in profound and lasting ways. Boards that frame cybersecurity solely as risk avoidance miss its moral dimension.

Ethical stewardship strengthens trust. Trust, once lost, is extraordinarily difficult to restore.

Cybersecurity governance that ignores ethics may satisfy formal requirements while undermining legitimacy.

Chapter 46: Privacy, Trust, and the Social License to Operate

Trust is an organizational asset, though it rarely appears on balance sheets.

Customers, donors, beneficiaries, partners, and the public grant organizations a form of social license: permission to operate, collect data, and provide services. Cybersecurity failures can erode this license rapidly and, in some cases, irreversibly.

Boards must understand that cybersecurity governance is a core component of trust governance. How an organization protects information, responds to incidents, and communicates transparently shapes stakeholder perceptions long after technical remediation is complete.

Regulatory compliance may prevent sanctions, but it does not guarantee trust. Trust is earned through consistent behavior over time.

Boards should therefore evaluate cybersecurity decisions not only through legal and financial lenses, but also through their impact on long-term credibility and stakeholder confidence.

Chapter 47: Psychological Safety, Reporting, and the Prevention of Silence

One of the most dangerous cultural failures in cybersecurity governance is the suppression of bad news.

Organizations rarely fail because no one knew about a problem. They fail because those who knew did not feel safe escalating it—or believed escalation would be futile.

Psychological safety is therefore a governance concern. Employees, managers, and technical staff must believe that reporting concerns, vulnerabilities, or incidents will be met with seriousness and support rather than blame or dismissal.

Boards influence psychological safety indirectly through their reactions. When Directors punish messengers, trivialize findings, or reward superficial optimism, silence becomes rational behavior.

Effective governance encourages early reporting, even when information is incomplete. It recognizes that uncertainty is inherent in cybersecurity and that delayed escalation often increases harm.

Silence is not neutrality. It is a risk multiplier.

Chapter 48: Resilience as a Cultural and Governance Outcome

Resilience is often described in technical terms: redundancy, backups, recovery time objectives. These elements matter, but they are insufficient without cultural alignment.

Resilient organizations share common cultural traits:

- willingness to acknowledge vulnerability,
- discipline in preparation,
- clarity in decision-making,
- adaptability under stress,
- commitment to learning after failure.

Boards shape resilience by governing for long-term capability rather than short-term comfort. This includes supporting investments that may not produce immediate returns but materially improve preparedness and recovery.

Resilience is not the absence of incidents. It is the capacity to absorb shock, recover function, and retain trust.

Cybersecurity governance that neglects culture produces brittle systems. Governance that integrates culture produces endurance.

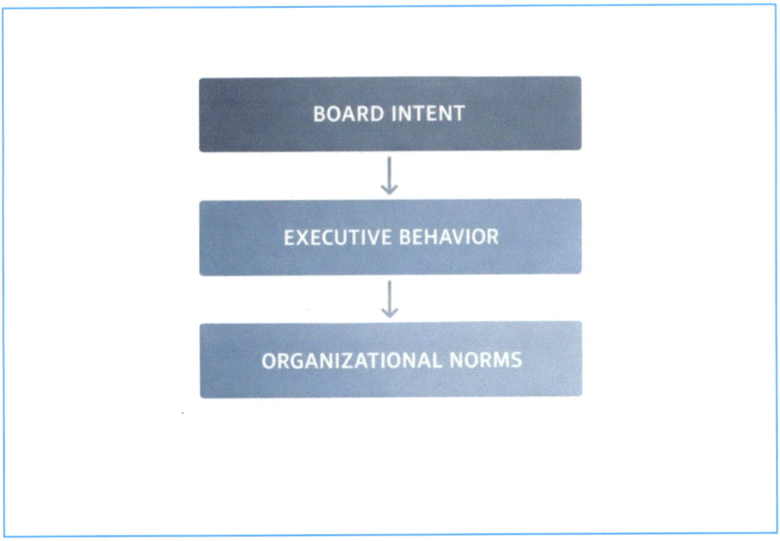

Culture and leadership is a "tone at the top" discussion

Closing of Part VIII

With Part VIII, the framework moves beyond structure and control into the human and ethical dimensions of governance.

At this point, the book has addressed:

- authority and accountability,
- risk and decision systems,
- policy and assurance,
- crisis leadership,
- extended enterprise exposure,
- and now culture, ethics, and trust.

What remains is the question of **evolution**: how Boards ensure that cybersecurity governance matures over time rather than stagnates.

That work is the focus of Part IX.

Part IX: Maturity, Strategic Evolution, and the Future of Cybersecurity Governance

Chapter 49: The Illusion of Cybersecurity Maturity

Few words in cybersecurity governance are used as casually—and as dangerously—as *maturity.*

Organizations often describe themselves as “mature” because they have implemented a framework, achieved a certification, or passed an audit. While these milestones may reflect progress, they do not necessarily indicate governance capability.

True maturity is not defined by artifacts. It is defined by **how reliably an organization identifies risk, makes decisions, adapts to change, and responds under pressure**.

Boards must be especially cautious of maturity claims that rely solely on checklists, scores, or self-assessments. Such indicators often measure conformity rather than effectiveness. They reward completion rather than judgment.

The illusion of maturity creates complacency. Complacency, in turn, blinds leadership to emerging risk. Many high-profile cyber failures occurred in organizations that believed themselves to be "advanced" or "well protected."

Governance maturity is not a destination. It is a discipline.

Chapter 50: Maturity Models as Governance Tools, Not Scorecards

Maturity models can be valuable—but only when used correctly.

At their best, maturity models provide a structured way to:

- understand current capability,
- identify gaps relative to risk,
- prioritize improvement efforts,
- communicate progress to leadership.

At their worst, they become scorecards that incentivize appearance over substance.

Boards should insist that maturity assessments be:

- grounded in **organizational context and risk**, not abstract benchmarks,
- externally validated or independently challenged,
- linked to decision-making and resource allocation,
- revisited regularly rather than treated as one-time exercises.

A maturity model that does not influence governance decisions is governance theater.

The purpose of maturity assessment is not to achieve the highest possible score. It is to ensure that capability aligns with risk and mission.

Chapter 51: Governance Drift and the Slow Erosion of Oversight

Governance rarely fails suddenly. More often, it erodes gradually.

As organizations grow, change leadership, adopt new technologies, or respond to external pressures, cybersecurity governance structures can drift from their original intent. Reporting becomes less rigorous. Policy reviews are delayed. Assurance findings are normalized. Escalation thresholds soften.

This drift is rarely malicious. It is usually the product of competing priorities and cognitive fatigue. Yet its consequences can be severe.

Boards must therefore treat governance maintenance as an ongoing responsibility. Structures that were appropriate three years ago may no longer be sufficient today. Assumptions that once held may no longer be valid.

Governance drift is difficult to detect from within. It requires periodic reflection, challenge, and renewal—often informed by independent perspective.

Boards that assume governance will sustain itself without attention are mistaken.

Chapter 52: Strategic Roadmapping for Cybersecurity Governance

Cybersecurity governance must evolve alongside organizational strategy.

Growth, digital transformation, mergers and acquisitions, regulatory change, and shifts in operating models all reshape cyber risk. Governance that does not adapt to these changes becomes misaligned and ineffective.

Boards should therefore require **multi-year cybersecurity governance roadmaps** that:

- anticipate strategic change,

- identify emerging risks,
- align capability development with organizational objectives,
- sequence investments deliberately.

These roadmaps should not be static plans. They should be living instruments, revisited and adjusted as conditions change.

Strategic roadmapping elevates cybersecurity governance from reactive defense to proactive stewardship.

Chapter 53:
Board Education and the Continuity of Oversight

Cybersecurity governance depends on informed oversight. Yet Boards are dynamic bodies. Directors rotate. New members arrive with different backgrounds. Institutional knowledge fades.

Without deliberate education and onboarding, cybersecurity oversight degrades over time.

Boards should treat cybersecurity literacy as a **continuity requirement**, not a one-time briefing. This includes:

- structured onboarding for new Directors,
- periodic education aligned to emerging risks,

- refreshers on governance roles and expectations.

Education does not mean turning Directors into technologists. It means equipping them to ask better questions, recognize warning signs, and exercise judgment.

A Board that does not invest in its own capability cannot govern cybersecurity credibly.

Chapter 54: Preparing for the Future Board Environment

The future governance environment will be more demanding, not less.

Regulatory expectations for Board oversight of cybersecurity continue to expand. Disclosure regimes are becoming more prescriptive. Stakeholders increasingly expect transparency and accountability. Technology dependency will deepen, not recede.

Boards that view cybersecurity governance as a temporary compliance challenge will struggle. Those that institutionalize it as a permanent discipline will adapt.

Future-ready Boards will:

- integrate cybersecurity into enterprise risk governance,
- maintain clear accountability and authority,
- demand evidence rather than reassurance,
- invest in resilience rather than optics,
- evolve governance as conditions change.

Cybersecurity governance is not about predicting the future. It is about building institutions capable of governing uncertainty.

Closing of Part IX

With Part IX, the framework confronts an uncomfortable truth: **governance that does not evolve will eventually fail.**

At this stage, the book has addressed:

- why cybersecurity is a Board responsibility,
- how governance structures are built,
- how risk is governed as a decision system,
- how policy establishes authority,
- how assurance validates effectiveness,
- how leadership performs under crisis,
- how ecosystems expand risk,
- how culture sustains or undermines governance,
- and now how maturity is maintained over time.

What remains is synthesis.

The final Part draws these threads together into a **Board-level cybersecurity playbook**—a practical, enduring framework for Directors and leaders navigating an insecure world.

Part X

The Board's Cybersecurity Playbook

Chapter 55: What Good Cybersecurity Governance Actually Looks Like

By the time a cyber incident reaches public view, governance quality has already determined the outcome.

Well-governed organizations are rarely distinguished by flawless prevention. They are distinguished by **clarity, discipline, and credibility**. Their Boards understand where responsibility lies. Leadership knows how decisions are made. Risk is surfaced early. Incidents are governed, not improvised.

Good cybersecurity governance is recognizable by several consistent traits.

First, **oversight is active but not intrusive.** Boards engage regularly, ask informed questions, and require evidence—without attempting to manage operations.

Second, **accountability is explicit.** Ownership of risk, authority for decisions, and responsibility for outcomes are clearly defined and understood.

Third, **risk is governed as risk**, not as technology. Decisions are framed in terms of impact, consequence, and trade-offs rather than tools and tactics.

Fourth, **assurance is independent and credible.** Leadership does not rely solely on self-reporting to validate effectiveness.

Finally, **documentation exists and matters.** Decisions, deliberations, and direction are recorded, creating an evidentiary trail of informed oversight.

These characteristics do not guarantee immunity from cyber incidents. They do, however, distinguish organizations that recover with trust intact from those that do not.

Chapter 56: The Board's Standing Responsibilities in Cybersecurity Oversight

Cybersecurity governance is not episodic. It does not occur only during audits, incidents, or regulatory examinations. It is a **standing responsibility** of the Board.

At a minimum, Boards should institutionalize the following recurring duties:

- **Regular oversight** of cyber risk posture and material exposures
- **Review and approval** of governance-level cybersecurity policies

- **Evaluation of assurance findings** and remediation progress
- **Engagement in preparedness activities**, including tabletop exercises
- **Periodic reassessment** of governance structures and maturity

These activities should be scheduled, documented, and revisited—not dependent on individual Director interest or management initiative.

Cybersecurity governance that relies on personality rather than structure is fragile. Institutionalization is the hallmark of maturity.

Chapter 57: Questions Effective Boards Ask—and Insist On Answering

Boards govern through inquiry. The quality of governance often correlates directly with the quality of questions asked.

Effective Boards consistently ask questions such as:

- What cyber risks could materially impair our mission or strategy?
- How do we know our controls and governance mechanisms are effective?
- Which risks are we explicitly accepting, and why?

- Where are we most dependent on third parties?
- How would leadership respond in the first 24 hours of a major incident?
- What assurance do we have that bad news will reach us early?

These questions are not technical. They are governance-grade.

Boards that avoid such questions out of discomfort or perceived complexity abdicate oversight. Boards that ask them regularly normalize accountability.

Good governance is not adversarial. It is inquisitive.

Chapter 58: Cybersecurity as an Enduring Board Discipline

One of the most dangerous assumptions Boards can make is that cybersecurity governance will eventually be “finished.”

It will not.

Technology will continue to evolve. Threat actors will adapt. Regulatory expectations will expand. Organizational dependencies will deepen. Each change introduces new risk dynamics.

Cybersecurity governance must therefore be treated as a **permanent Board discipline**, comparable to financial oversight, audit, and enterprise risk management.

This requires:

- sustained education and literacy,
- continuity planning for Board turnover,
- periodic reassessment of governance structures,
- willingness to challenge assumptions.

Boards that treat cybersecurity as a passing compliance phase will repeatedly relearn painful lessons. Boards that institutionalize it as a discipline will adapt.

Chapter 59: Defensibility, Not Perfection

This framework does not promise perfect security. No credible governance framework can.

Instead, it seeks to establish **defensible governance**—a standard that recognizes uncertainty while demanding diligence, judgment, and accountability.

Defensible governance means:

- leadership understood the risk,
- oversight structures existed and functioned,
- decisions were informed and documented,
- assurance mechanisms were in place,
- response was governed, not improvised.

In regulatory and legal contexts, this distinction matters profoundly. Organizations are rarely judged solely on outcomes. They are judged on whether leadership acted reasonably given what was known at the time.

Defensibility is the realistic goal of cybersecurity governance.

Chapter 60: Governing in an Insecure World

Cyber insecurity is now a permanent feature of organizational life.

Boards do not have the luxury of choosing whether to engage. They can only choose **how deliberately and how responsibly** they will govern.

This book has argued that cybersecurity is not a technical specialty to be delegated and forgotten. It is a governance responsibility that touches fiduciary duty, enterprise risk, ethics, culture, and trust.

Boards that embrace this responsibility position their organizations to endure disruption, recover from failure, and retain legitimacy. Boards that do not may discover—often suddenly—that governance gaps are far more damaging than technical ones.

Cybersecurity governance is not about fear. It is about stewardship.

In an insecure world, stewardship is leadership's highest calling.

From Obligation to Practice

This book began with a simple premise: **cybersecurity readiness is a governance responsibility**.

Across ten parts, it has shown how that responsibility is recognized, structured, exercised, validated, and sustained. It has demonstrated that cybersecurity governance is neither abstract nor optional. It is practical, documentable, and increasingly expected.

For Boards willing to engage seriously, cybersecurity governance becomes not a burden, but a source of organizational strength—clarifying authority, improving decision-making, and reinforcing trust.

The work does not end here. Governance never does.

But with this framework, Boards have a map.

The remaining choice is whether to follow it.

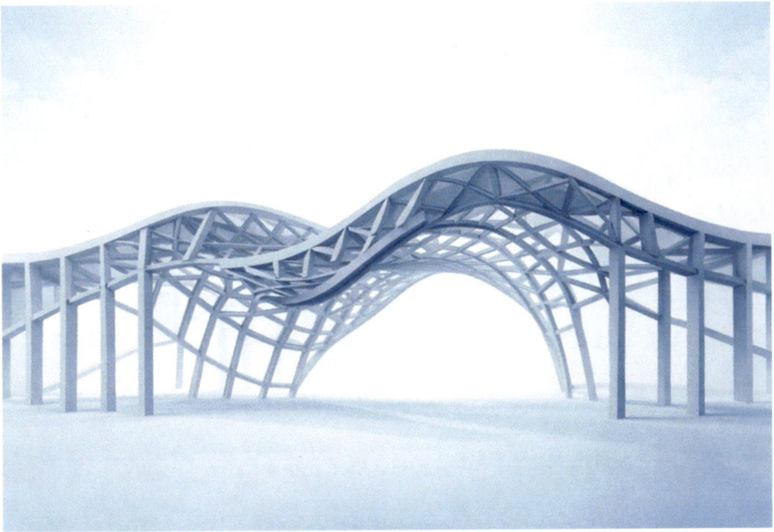

An architectural resilience metaphor: A system designed to flex, not resist.

References and Citations

Cybersecurity Governance, Oversight, and Fiduciary Responsibility

I. U.S. Federal Standards and Frameworks

National Institute of Standards and Technology

National Institute of Standards and Technology. *Cybersecurity Framework (CSF) 2.0*. Gaithersburg, MD: NIST, 2024.

National Institute of Standards and Technology. *Framework for Improving Critical Infrastructure Cybersecurity*, Version 1.1. Gaithersburg, MD: NIST, 2018.

National Institute of Standards and Technology. *Managing Information Security Risk: Organization,*

Mission, and Information System View (SP 800-39). Gaithersburg, MD: NIST, 2011.

National Institute of Standards and Technology. *Security and Privacy Controls for Information Systems and Organizations (SP 800-53 Rev. 5).* Gaithersburg, MD: NIST, 2020.

National Institute of Standards and Technology. *Risk Management Framework for Information Systems and Organizations (SP 800-37 Rev. 2).* Gaithersburg, MD: NIST, 2018.

Governance relevance:
NIST publications establish the de facto U.S. benchmark for risk-based cybersecurity governance. Courts and regulators frequently cite them as evidence of "reasonable" practices, even for non-federal entities.

II. International Standards

International Organization for Standardization

International Organization for Standardization. *ISO/IEC 27001:2022 — Information Security, Cybersecurity and Privacy Protection — Information Security Management Systems — Requirements*. Geneva: ISO, 2022.

International Organization for Standardization. *ISO/IEC 27002:2022 — Information Security Controls*. Geneva: ISO, 2022.

International Organization for Standardization. *ISO 31000:2018 — Risk Management — Guidelines*. Geneva: ISO, 2018.

International Organization for Standardization. *ISO/IEC 27014:2020 — Governance of Information Security*. Geneva: ISO, 2020.

Governance relevance:

ISO standards explicitly link cybersecurity to organizational governance, risk management, and leadership accountability, reinforcing the Board-level framing used throughout this book.

III. U.S. Securities Regulation and Disclosure

U.S. Securities and Exchange Commission

U.S. Securities and Exchange Commission. *Cybersecurity Risk Management, Strategy, Governance, and Incident Disclosure*. Final Rule, Release No. 33-11216. Washington, DC: SEC, July 26, 2023.

U.S. Securities and Exchange Commission. *Commission Statement and Guidance on Public Company Cybersecurity Disclosures*. Release Nos. 33-10459; 34-82746. Washington, DC: SEC, 2018.

U.S. Securities and Exchange Commission. *Sample Letter to Companies Regarding Cybersecurity Disclosures*. Washington, DC: SEC Division of Corporation Finance, 2021.

Governance relevance:

SEC rules and guidance make Board oversight of cybersecurity governance explicit, including disclosure of Board expertise, governance processes, and material incident response.

IV. U.S. Department of Justice and Enforcement Guidance

U.S. Department of Justice

U.S. Department of Justice. *Evaluation of Corporate Compliance Programs*. Updated guidance. Washington, DC: DOJ Criminal Division, March 2023.

U.S. Department of Justice. *Civil Cyber-Fraud Initiative*. Washington, DC: DOJ, 2021.

U.S. Department of Justice. *Cybersecurity Incident Response Guide for the Public and Private Sectors.* Washington, DC: DOJ, CISA, and FBI, 2020.

Governance relevance:
DOJ guidance explicitly evaluates whether Boards and senior leadership exercised oversight, resourced compliance programs, and responded appropriately to known risks—principles mirrored throughout this framework.

—

V. State-Level and Fiduciary Case Law

Delaware Court of Chancery

In re Caremark International Inc. Derivative Litigation, 698 A.2d 959 (Del. Ch. 1996).

Stone v. Ritter, 911 A.2d 362 (Del. 2006).

Marchand v. Barnhill, 212 A.3d 805 (Del. 2019).

In re Boeing Company Derivative Litigation, 2021 WL 4059934 (Del. Ch. Sept. 7, 2021).

Governance relevance:

These cases establish and reaffirm Board duties of oversight, particularly regarding mission-critical risk. Courts increasingly analogize cybersecurity to other core compliance and safety risks discussed in these decisions.

VI. Federal Trade Commission and Consumer Protection

Federal Trade Commission

Federal Trade Commission. *Protecting Personal Information: A Guide for Business*. Washington, DC: FTC, 2023.

Federal Trade Commission. *FTC v. Wyndham Worldwide Corp.*, 799 F.3d 236 (3d Cir. 2015).

Federal Trade Commission. *FTC Safeguards Rule*, 16 CFR Part 314, amended 2021.

Governance relevance:

FTC enforcement consistently frames cybersecurity failures as unreasonable governance and risk management practices, not merely technical errors.

VII. Insurance, Audit, and Risk Governance Sources

Committee of Sponsoring Organizations of the Treadway Commission (COSO). *Enterprise Risk Management — Integrating with Strategy and Performance*. Durham, NC: COSO, 2017.

Public Company Accounting Oversight Board. *Auditing Accounting Estimates and Related Disclosures (AS 2501)*. Washington, DC: PCAOB, 2018.

Public Company Accounting Oversight Board. *The Auditor's Responsibilities Relating to Other Information (AS 2710)*. Washington, DC: PCAOB, 2010.

Governance relevance:

COSO and PCAOB materials reinforce the integration of cybersecurity into enterprise risk management and oversight evidence relied upon by Boards and auditors.

VIII. Supplemental Governance and Board Guidance

National Association of Corporate Directors. *Cyber-Risk Oversight Handbook*. Washington, DC: NACD, 2020.

World Economic Forum. *Principles for Board Governance of Cyber Risk*. Geneva: WEF, 2018.

OECD. *Digital Security Risk Management for Economic and Social Prosperity*. Paris: OECD Publishing, 2015.

Governance relevance:

These sources reflect emerging global consensus that cybersecurity oversight is a Board-level responsibility grounded in fiduciary governance, not technical administration.

How These References Are Used in This Book

This book does not quote standards verbatim or prescribe compliance with any single framework. Instead, it synthesizes **shared governance expectations** that recur across:

- NIST and ISO risk frameworks
- SEC disclosure and governance rules
- DOJ compliance and enforcement doctrine
- Fiduciary duty case law
- Audit and enterprise risk standards

The result is a **framework-agnostic but regulator-aligned governance model**, suitable for organizations across sectors.

Regulatory Alignment Matrix

This is a **Board- and regulator-ready Regulatory Alignment Matrix**, mapping **each major chapter domain** to the **authoritative standards, regulatory expectations, and case law** it relies upon.

This matrix is designed to be:

- used by **auditors, regulators, grant monitors, and counsel**,
- defensible as an articulation of *"authorities relied upon"* for governance decisions.

It deliberately maps at the **chapter / governance-domain level**, not individual sentences, which is how regulators and courts evaluate oversight.

Cybersecurity as a Governance Responsibility

Part I — Cybersecurity as a Governance Obligation

Chapter	Governance Focus	Primary Authority	Key Citations
Ch. 1 – End of Cybersecurity as a Technical Problem	Cyber as governance responsibility	National Institute of Standards and Technology	NIST CSF 2.0 (2024); NIST SP 800-39
Ch. 2 – Cyber Risk as Enterprise Risk	Enterprise risk framing	Committee of Sponsoring Organizations of the Treadway Commission	COSO ERM (2017); ISO 31000
Ch. 3 – Fiduciary Duty in the Cyber Age	Duty of oversight	Delaware Court of Chancery	*Caremark*; *Stone v. Ritter*; *Marchand v. Barnhill*
Ch. 4 – Cybersecurity and Mission Failure	Mission-critical risk	Delaware case law; DOJ	*Marchand*; DOJ Compliance Guidance (2023)

Part II — Governance Architecture for Cybersecurity

Chapter	Governance Focus	Primary Authority	Key Citations
Ch. 5 – Governing vs Managing	Oversight vs execution	International Organization for Standardization	ISO/IEC 27014
Ch. 6 – Governance Model	Three lines of defense	ISO; COSO	ISO 27001; COSO ERM
Ch. 7 – Roles & Authority	Accountability clarity	DOJ; SEC	DOJ Evaluation of Compliance Programs
Ch. 8 – Committees & Reporting	Board structures	U.S. Securities and Exchange Commission	SEC Cyber Governance Rule (2023)
Ch. 9 – Information Flow & Escalation	Escalation discipline	DOJ; NIST	DOJ Compliance Guidance; NIST CSF
Ch. 10 – Governance Failure Modes	Oversight breakdowns	Delaware case law	*Boeing Derivative Litigation*

Part III — Cyber Risk as a Board-Level System

Chapter	Governance Focus	Primary Authority	Key Citations
Ch. 11 – Risk Framing	Decision-grade risk	NIST; ISO	NIST SP 800-39; ISO 31000
Ch. 12 – Risk Appetite	Risk tolerance	SEC; COSO	SEC Disclosure Guidance; COSO ERM
Ch. 13 – Risk Assessment	Enterprise assessment	NIST	NIST CSF; NIST SP 800-53
Ch. 14 – Risk Treatment	Acceptance & mitigation	DOJ; ISO	DOJ Compliance Guidance; ISO 27001
Ch. 15 – Investment Governance	Risk-aligned spend	SEC; DOJ	SEC Cyber Rule; DOJ
Ch. 16 – Risk Ownership	Accountability	Delaware case law	*Caremark*; *Stone v. Ritter*

Part IV — Policy as a Governance Instrument

Chapter	Governance Focus	Primary Authority	Key Citations
Ch. 17 - Policy Authority	Policy as governance	ISO	ISO/IEC 27001
Ch. 18 - Policy Hierarchy	Board-level policy	SEC; ISO	SEC Cyber Rule; ISO 27014
Ch. 19 - Core Policies	Required governance set	NIST; FTC	NIST CSF; FTC Safeguards Rule
Ch. 20 - Policy as Evidence	Due diligence proof	DOJ; FTC	DOJ Compliance Guidance
Ch. 21 - Policy Lifecycle	Governance drift	ISO	ISO 27001
Ch. 22 - Exceptions & Enforcement	Discipline	DOJ	DOJ Compliance Guidance

Part V — Assurance, Oversight, and Monitoring

Chapter	Governance Focus	Primary Authority	Key Citations
Ch. 23 - Assurance vs Activity	Effectiveness validation	Public Company Accounting Oversight Board	PCAOB AS 2501
Ch. 24 - Independent Validation	Independence	PCAOB; ISO	PCAOB standards; ISO 27001
Ch. 25 - Audit & Oversight	Assurance reporting	PCAOB	AS 2710
Ch. 26 - Metrics	Decision-useful metrics	SEC; NIST	SEC Cyber Rule; NIST CSF
Ch. 27 - Continuous Monitoring	Feedback loops	NIST	NIST CSF
Ch. 28 - Transparency	Escalation culture	DOJ	DOJ Compliance Guidance

Part VI — Incident Preparedness and Leadership

Decision-Making

Chapter	Governance Focus	Primary Authority	Key Citations
Ch. 29 - Incidents as Crises	Crisis governance	DOJ; SEC	DOJ IR Guide; SEC Disclosure Rule
Ch. 30 - Preparedness	Pre-incident governance	NIST	NIST CSF Respond/Recover
Ch. 31 - Decision Rights	Authority clarity	DOJ	DOJ Compliance Guidance
Ch. 32 - Board Role in Incidents	Oversight conduct	SEC; Delaware courts	SEC Rule; *Caremark*
Ch. 33 - Legal & Disclosure	Regulatory response	SEC	SEC Cyber Rule
Ch. 34 - Tabletop Exercises	Governance testing	NIST; DOJ	NIST CSF
Ch. 35 - Post-Incident Review	Learning & remediation	DOJ	DOJ Compliance Guidance

Part VII — Third-Party and Ecosystem Risk

Chapter	Governance Focus	Primary Authority	Key Citations
Ch. 36 – Boundary Myth	Extended enterprise	NIST	NIST CSF
Ch. 37 – Ecosystem Risk	Vendor exposure	FTC	FTC v. Wyndham
Ch. 38 – Due Diligence	Risk-based vetting	DOJ; ISO	DOJ Compliance Guidance
Ch. 39 – Contractual Controls	Governance limits	FTC	FTC enforcement actions
Ch. 40 – Ongoing Monitoring	Dynamic risk	NIST	NIST CSF
Ch. 41 – Dependency & Exit	Concentration risk	SEC; DOJ	SEC risk disclosure
Ch. 42 – Accountability	Non-delegable duty	Delaware case law	*Marchand*

Part VIII — Culture, Ethics, and Resilience

Chapter	Governance Focus	Primary Authority	Key Citations
Ch. 43 - Culture	Board tone	DOJ	DOJ Compliance Guidance
Ch. 44 - Tone at the Top	Behavioral signals	DOJ	DOJ
Ch. 45 - Ethics & Stewardship	Moral obligation	OECD	OECD Digital Security Risk
Ch. 46 - Trust & Privacy	Social license	FTC	FTC enforcement
Ch. 47 - Psychological Safety	Escalation culture	DOJ	DOJ
Ch. 48 - Resilience	Endurance	NIST	NIST CSF Recover

Part IX — Maturity and Strategic Evolution

Chapter	Governance Focus	Primary Authority	Key Citations
Ch. 49 - Maturity Illusion	False confidence	ISO; NIST	ISO 27001; NIST
Ch. 50 - Maturity Models	Governance tools	ISO	ISO 27001
Ch. 51 - Governance Drift	Oversight erosion	Delaware case law	*Boeing*
Ch. 52 - Strategic Roadmaps	Long-term planning	COSO	COSO ERM
Ch. 53 - Board Education	Oversight continuity	SEC	SEC Cyber Rule
Ch. 54 - Future Board	Evolving duty	SEC; DOJ	SEC; DOJ

Part X — The Board's Cybersecurity Playbook

Chapter	Governance Focus	Primary Authority	Key Citations
Ch. 55 - Good Governance	Oversight standards	Delaware courts	*Caremark* line
Ch. 56 - Standing Duties	Institutionalization	SEC	SEC Cyber Rule
Ch. 57 - Board Questions	Inquiry standard	DOJ	DOJ Compliance
Ch. 58 - Enduring Discipline	Permanent duty	ISO; SEC	ISO 27014
Ch. 59 - Defensibility	Reasonableness	Case law; DOJ	*Stone v. Ritter*
Ch. 60 - Stewardship	Governance synthesis	All above	Integrated

How This Matrix Is Intended to Be Used

- **Boards:** demonstrate informed reliance on recognized authorities
- **Auditors & regulators:** trace governance expectations to sources
- **Counsel:** support reasonableness and duty-of-care arguments
- **Grant monitors:** map to federal internal control expectations

This matrix makes explicit what regulators already assume implicitly:

cybersecurity governance is judged by alignment to established authority, not by technical novelty.

JURISDICTION-SPECIFIC ADDENDA

Applying the Governance Framework to Sector-Specific Legal and Regulatory Expectations

Addendum A: Nonprofit Organizations

A1. Regulatory and Oversight Reality for Nonprofits

Nonprofits are often treated as "informal" from a governance standpoint, but their cyber obligations are frequently more complex than similarly sized for-profit businesses because they combine:

- donor and payment data
- beneficiary/client data (often sensitive)
- federal and state grant requirements
- third-party ecosystems (case management, fundraising platforms, cloud services)

For nonprofits, cybersecurity scrutiny typically arises through three channels:

1. **Grant and federal award monitoring** (internal controls, documentation, procurement, subrecipient oversight)
2. **State enforcement and breach response** (breach notification and consumer protection expectations vary by state)
3. **Vendor and contractual compliance** (service providers impose security obligations; insurers increasingly demand formal programs)

A2. Primary Authorities and What They Imply

2 CFR 200.303 (Uniform Guidance) – Internal Controls requires recipients and subrecipients to establish, document, and maintain effective internal control over federal awards.
This is not "financial only." It is operational governance. If cybersecurity failures can impair program delivery or compliance, they are an internal control concern.

COSO ERM alignment is frequently used as the internal control reference point for governance expectations in audit and monitoring contexts (especially when paired with Uniform Guidance's internal control language). (COSO was already referenced in the core References section.)

A3. Board-Level Expectations to Institutionalize

Nonprofit boards should formalize cybersecurity governance as part of fiduciary stewardship by adopting:

- a Board-approved **information security governance policy** (authority + accountability)
- a Board-level **risk appetite statement** for sensitive beneficiary/donor data and mission-critical operations
- a standing **cyber risk reporting cadence** (quarterly minimum, plus incident-driven briefings)

- explicit **vendor/third-party risk oversight** for fundraising platforms, case management, and cloud hosting

A4. Minimum Governance Artifacts for Nonprofits

Nonprofits relying on this framework should treat the following as “defensibility minimums”:

- Cybersecurity Governance Charter (Board/committee scope, reporting cadence)
- Information Security Policy (governance-level)
- Data Classification & Handling Policy (donor/beneficiary emphasis)
- Incident Response Policy + Breach Notification Protocol (state-specific appendix as needed)
- Third-Party & Vendor Risk Policy (including subrecipient/vendor data handling)
- Annual cybersecurity readiness attestation package for grant files (policy adoption,

training completion, tabletop exercise summary, risk register excerpt)

A5. Practical Implementation Note

A nonprofit does not need enterprise tooling to achieve enterprise-grade governance. What it does need is discipline: clarity of authority, documented oversight, and evidence of follow-through.

Addendum B: Healthcare Organizations

B1. Why Healthcare Is a Special Governance Environment

Healthcare cybersecurity is governed under an assumption that failures can create immediate and severe harm—privacy violations, clinical disruption, delayed care, and patient safety impacts. The sector is also uniquely exposed to ransomware and extortion.

Healthcare boards must govern cybersecurity not only as information protection, but as a **care-delivery resilience requirement**.

B2. Primary Authorities and What They Imply

HIPAA Security Rule (45 CFR Part 164 Subpart C) requires administrative safeguards including **risk analysis** and **risk management**, explicitly requiring an accurate and thorough assessment of risks to electronic protected health information (ePHI) and measures sufficient to reduce risk to a reasonable and appropriate level.

HIPAA Breach Notification Rule (45 CFR 164.400–414) requires notification following breaches of unsecured PHI, with explicit obligations applying to covered entities and business associates.

These requirements collectively imply a governance posture where:

- risk assessment is continuous and documented
- incident response is pre-governed (not improvised)
- vendor/business associate governance is mandatory, not optional

B3. Board-Level Expectations to Institutionalize

Healthcare boards should require:

- a formal **ePHI-focused risk analysis cadence** with documented remediation prioritization
- a Board-visible **clinical downtime and continuity posture** (recovery objectives are governance decisions)
- Board participation in at least annual **incident and downtime tabletop exercises**
- a governed approach to **business associates** (assurance evidence, notification timelines, termination/exit planning)

B4. Healthcare-Specific Governance Artifacts

In addition to the core suite, healthcare organizations should maintain:

- ePHI Risk Analysis Methodology + Report Template (repeatable, auditable)

- Business Associate Security Addendum Standard (contract + assurance expectations)
- Clinical Downtime Governance Protocol (decision rights, escalation, communications)
- Breach Notification Decision Tree (legal/regulatory + stakeholder communications)

B5. Practical Implementation Note

In healthcare, cyber resilience is operational resilience. Governance should explicitly tie security preparedness to continuity of care and patient trust, not merely "IT compliance."

Addendum C: Financial Services

C1. Why Financial Services Is Governed More Aggressively

Financial services cybersecurity is treated as systemic risk: disruption can affect markets, consumer welfare, and critical infrastructure. Scrutiny tends to be prescriptive and enforcement-oriented, with heightened expectations for board involvement, testing, and vendor control.

C2. Primary Authorities and What They Imply

SEC Cybersecurity Disclosure Rule (Release No. 33-11216) requires public companies to make structured disclosures regarding cybersecurity risk management, strategy, and governance and to report material incidents on Form 8-K within specified timing once materiality is determined.

FTC Safeguards Rule guidance (GLBA-related for FTC-jurisdiction institutions) requires a Qualified Individual and includes expectations for written reporting to the board or governing body at least annually.
(Effective-date and implementation reminders are often reinforced in sector communications tied to the Safeguards Rule updates.)

NYDFS 23 NYCRR 500 (for covered entities) includes amended cybersecurity regulation requirements with phased compliance timelines under the 2023 amendments.

Collectively, these drive three governance realities:

- Board visibility into cyber governance must be demonstrable, not informal
- incident materiality and disclosure governance must be pre-planned

- third-party governance is treated as a first-order risk domain

C3. Board-Level Expectations to Institutionalize

Financial services boards should require:

- formalized **materiality determination and escalation procedures** (integrated with legal and disclosure)
- an annual **board cybersecurity report** from the designated security leader/Qualified Individual (content requirements should include program status, control effectiveness, and material risk posture)
- disciplined **vendor concentration and exit risk governance**, particularly for cloud and managed services
- independent assurance including penetration tests, control testing, and governance validation at regular intervals

C4. Financial Services-Specific Governance Artifacts

Add to the core suite:

- SEC Incident Materiality and Disclosure Playbook (roles, thresholds, evidence preservation)
- Annual Board Cybersecurity Report Template (Qualified Individual format)
- NYDFS Part 500 Compliance Mapping Appendix (if applicable)
- Vendor Concentration Risk Register + Exit/Transition Plans for critical providers

C5. Practical Implementation Note

In financial services, “reasonable security” is judged by **governance evidence**: structured reporting, documented decisions, independent validation, and disciplined incident governance.

Addendum D: Public Sector and Government-Adjacent Organizations

D1. Scope Clarification

This addendum applies to:

- federal agencies and federal contractors
- state and local government entities
- nonprofits and vendors operating as **recipients/subrecipients** of federal funds
- organizations handling **Controlled Unclassified Information (CUI)** or operating within federal program ecosystems

D2. Primary Authorities and What They Imply

2 CFR 200.303 (Uniform Guidance) requires documented internal controls over federal awards.

OMB Circular A-130 establishes federal policy for information governance, security, and privacy and emphasizes risk-based, continuous programs rather than compliance-only approaches.

FISMA (Federal Information Security Modernization Act) establishes federal information security governance expectations and ties to the NIST standards ecosystem.

CISA Binding Operational Directive 22-01 establishes requirements for remediation of known exploited vulnerabilities for covered federal environments and creates governance urgency around vulnerability prioritization.

FedRAMP provides the standardized federal approach to cloud security authorization and continuous monitoring, built on NIST baselines and structured assessment expectations.

NIST SP 800-171 Rev. 3 provides recommended security requirements for protecting the confidentiality of CUI in nonfederal systems and organizations.

D3. Board and Leadership Expectations to Institutionalize

For public sector entities and government-adjacent organizations, governance should explicitly require:

- documented internal controls that treat cybersecurity as program integrity, not IT hygiene
- formal risk management aligned to NIST-style controls and continuous monitoring doctrine
- disciplined vulnerability management governance that prioritizes known exploited vulnerabilities
- cloud authorization governance aligned to FedRAMP expectations where applicable

- CUI handling governance where applicable, including supplier and subcontractor controls

D4. Public Sector-Specific Governance Artifacts

In addition to the core suite, maintain:

- Federal Awards Cyber Internal Control Appendix (2 CFR 200.303 alignment)
- CUI Handling Standard + Flowdown Clauses (if CUI is in scope)
- KEV/Vulnerability Governance SOP (prioritization, deadlines, escalation)
- Cloud Authorization & Continuous Monitoring Governance Procedure (FedRAMP-aligned where relevant)
- System/Service Inventory Governance Protocol (ownership, classification, reporting)

D5. Practical Implementation Note

Public sector cybersecurity governance is evaluated as **program stewardship**. Auditors and oversight bodies tend to focus less on sophistication and more on: documented controls, repeatable process, evidence of monitoring, and corrective action discipline.

Made in the USA
Las Vegas, NV
03 November 2026

57420357R00138